FENG SHUI

The Book of Cures

FENG SHUI

The Book of Cures

150 Simple Solutions for Health and Happiness in Your Home or Office

Nancilee Wydra

CB
CONTEMPORARY BOOKS
A TRIBUNE COMPANY

Library of Congress Cataloging-in-Publication Data

Wydra, Nancilee.
Feng shui : the book of cures : 150 simple solutions for health and happiness in your home or office / Nancilee Wydra ; illustrations by Samuel Angus Welborn.
p. cm.
ISBN 0-8092-3168-9
1. Feng-shui. I. Title.
BF1779.F4W93 1996
133.3′33—dc20 96-13806
CIP

Cover design by Kim Bartko
Front cover photo courtesy Lindal Cedar Homes, Inc., Seattle, Washington, 1-800-426-0536
Back cover photos (top) Sharon Hoogstraten, (bottom) © Peter Pearson/Tony Stone Images
Interior design by Mary Lockwood
Interior art by Samuel Angus Welborn, Route 7, Box 67, Jasper, GA 30143
Author photo by cōleen nēeld

Published by Contemporary Books
An imprint of NTC/Contemporary Publishing Company
Two Prudential Plaza, Chicago, Illinois 60601-6790
Manufactured in the United States of America
International Standard Book Number: 0-8092-3168-9

10 9 8 7 6 5 4 3 2 1

To my husband, Bill, whose inspiration, patience, loyalty, values, disposition, academic rigorousness, and love have all added immeasurably to my life.

To Zachary, Robyn, Sol and Vera, Steve and Melissa, Sandy Vidan, Sandy and Milt Thomas, Faith Mitchell, Brenda Currin, Karen Amsler, Susan Carver, Willie Goodman, Jean Nidorf, Elizabeth Freilicher, Ethel Marantz, Diana Helman, Joanne Huot, Jackie Stern, Anita Goldberg, Millie Levinstone, Micki Wesson, Ethel Weinstein, and my wonderful clients—whose lives intertwine with mine and whose stories I tell.

And to Miss Goodyear, my tenth-grade English teacher, who dared to believe in me. Her gift is lifelong.

Contents

FENG SHUI

The Book of Cures

INTRODUCTION

Feng shui explains the dialogue enacted every day between you and your living spaces. While architecture and interior design are concerned with aesthetics, feng shui focuses on how an environment is experienced by the people who inhabit it. Harmonious living spaces can add measurably to life's satisfactions; that premise is at the heart of feng shui. You may have read myriad magazine or newspaper articles that have conveyed this definition and yet still not have a true understanding of how to adjust an environment to benefit your own life. If you're interested in evaluating your living space and then selecting the best cures for the problems you identify, this book is for you.

Feng Shui: The Book of Cures can be used as an encyclopedia. Read Part I for background or, if you prefer, go straight to Part II and choose the chapters of interest. The test at the beginning of each chapter will help you decide how to adjust that part of your home or office. You'll find that correcting unfavorable conditions is often simple and inexpensive.

Although feng shui originated thousands of years ago in China, the core truths can be applied to any civilization. Nothing lasts that long unless its truths are as central to human awareness and experience as the heart is to a physical body. And when stripped of the customs and rituals peculiar to China, feng shui emerges as solid and essential to all human experience as addition and subtraction are to all mathematics. We are all awed by sights like the Grand Canyon or Niagara Falls. All humans respond physically to light and dark in the same way. What must be stripped away from this ancient discipline are the garnishes, the cultural spices that make each civilization a feast of nuances. This book looks toward the universal message contained inside feng shui.

Best future!
Nancilee Wydra

Part I

Feng Shui: The Person-Place Connection

1

Power of Place

I can recall how places felt to me as a child. On my way to school each morning my girlfriends and I walked past our neighborhood's "haunted house." The early morning sun peeping up from behind this home's conical roof created an ominous shadow on the cracked cement sidewalk.

We brooded about the folks who lived there, mainly because no one ever saw them except for brief glimpses at dusk, when they returned from parts unknown. Hot summer weekends would come and go, but the haunted-house family was never like other folks, relaxing on backyard plastic-slatted lounge chairs. In winter a local plow service would clear the driveway after an abundant snowfall, but this reclusive family left the front steps unshoveled. When they finally moved away, the strangest thing happened. The family that replaced them was also odd. I remember wondering then if it was perhaps the house that caused these families to be strange.

Looking back, I realize this house had terrible feng shui. It was at the end of a T-juncture in a roadway and had an enormous dead tree stump stationed like a wounded sentinel by the front door. Buildings at the end of a T-juncture can suffer the negative effect of racing energy as cars, people, or wind drives straight down the unencumbered roadway toward them. Not removing a

A house at the end of a T-juncture

dead tree stump signals a family's lack of sensitivity to its surroundings. If we don't take care of that which once radiated life, there is a great likelihood that we will be careless with our own well-being.

Much more recently, I lectured at a popular holistic health center. The founder had stepped down and the organizational glue was dissipating. As soon as I arrived, I identified the stench of decline by observing the physical plant. Formerly a pristine environment, it was fraught with tiny enclaves of clutter, litter, and disrepair.

A family, person, or institution's health can be detected by interpreting conditions in an environment. Our relationship with our surroundings is interactive, and the health of one is reflected in the other. Even small changes can consume vitality like a rotten apple in a barrel of healthy ones.

As contemporary Westerners, however, we must relearn that biology, social structure, and psychology flavor the soup of human individuality. We ignore how our ancestors lived for thousands of generations. No longer do we time our waking and sleeping patterns with the rising and setting of the sun. We create uniformly lit spaces with no regard for the normal changes in daylight. This requires our bodies to keep a steady pace all day long rather than rise and ebb with the passage of light. We are both blessed and cursed with the power to interact with our environment unlike any other species. Sensitivity to our internal condition is weakened when we allow technology to overwhelm biology.

To understand the philosophy behind feng shui, a knowledge of how we are tied biologically to our environment is imperative. Just as we are molded by the people who rear us, we are shaped by the sensory interactions between us and our setting.

In a trailblazing experiment during the 1960s social scientist Roger Barker recorded the actions of children in different venues over an extended period of time. The results were astonishing. In a line at a movie theater, an aggressive child would wait submissively, for example, while at a football game a normally subdued child would shout with abandon. Barker concluded that the places children occupied influenced their behavior more than any other factor, including their own personalities.

We see similar patterns in our own lives. Just think about how you shift your persona depending on whether you're in a doctor's office, buying a car, or acting as host to guests in your home. Such interactions are inescapable, so it's no surprise that from Barker's groundbreaking work evolved a new field of study called *psychological ecology*, a field in which feng shui has much to offer.

We can consider ourselves addicted to our environment in the same way as a drug addict is addicted to drugs. When studying addicts' recidivism rate, Shepard Siegel, a professor of psychology at McMaster University in Hamilton, Ontario, found that even those with great resolve to quit after having successfully completed a drying-out program would resume their habit upon returning to the setting in which it began. In the same way as Pavlov's dogs salivated after hearing a bell ring, an alcoholic's craving could be triggered just by driving by a favorite bar. Most of us have experienced a surge in appetite when we were not hungry, just because food is placed before us.

On a very deep level our environment triggers automatic responses. These involuntary actions emerge from the part of the brain that handles routine things like running down a flight of stairs without thinking "Now I bend my knee, now I straighten my knee," etc. We are not aware of the specifics that propel a response. All of us have, at one time or another, experienced extreme elation or anxiety when entering a particular place, and more often than not we are unaware of the particular factors that precipitate these feelings. The part of our brain responding to these stimuli is the brain stem, which houses our ancient memory, the collective programming embedded in our response system, like fight-or-flight response.

We breathe, feel, smell, see, and respond to our environment through the responses of our psychological/biological selves; we depend on these predictable sets of responses to our surroundings to live collectively. It's not by chance that neighborhoods tend to resemble each other or that buildings have many design elements in common. Before literacy was widespread, cities and buildings needed to be constructed in ways that could be recalled from house to house and from city to city. Quintilian, a Roman architect, wrote that "a building is to be remembered. . . ." He suggested standardizing positioning of courtyards, living rooms, bedrooms, and parlors so that people could navigate without having to discover the layout every time they entered a different building. By complying to the dictates of a culture's norms, we create a tolerable, predictable world in which to live.

In a positive way this conformity of place or environmental addiction keeps people rooted. The recent trend that catapults more than one million families a year to new locations is perhaps a factor compelling us to homogenize America. Perhaps we feel comfortable moving so often only because we have created such a uniform world.

But the pressure to conform to the status quo of place has a downside as well. Habituation makes it difficult for us to adapt to a new environment when we must. During my childhood, when my family drove to Florida from New Jersey, the foods, sights, and sounds in the southern towns along the way seemed as exotic to me as in any foreign country. The route we traveled was diverse, visually and culturally as well as climatically. I realized that being transplanted could be as tough as learning a new language. Even those who love to travel return home with a "Wow, I'm glad to be home" feeling.

The very instinct that helps us establish strong roots also keeps us rooted when that's the last thing we need. So entrenched are we in the status quo that we are loath to change our environment when our needs change. People who linger in a large home after the children leave or stay near a job site after retirement often experience a nagging depression or feeling of loss. The act of changing environments can be the single most important cure for this condition. My home state of Florida is deluged with people who have made such a transition.

We often fail to recognize how a change in lifestyle or life stage is affecting our experience in our surroundings. We may be even less aware of the subtle influences our physical world has on us. Be it electromagnetic fields, geophysical energies, or other properties, the contents of an environment exert power to alter any experience. For example, the negative ions created by water infuse us and the air around us with an exhilarating positive energy. On some level we apparently know this because real estate close to water tends to command the highest price. But we don't always consciously take it into account in manipulating our environments to suit us.

Robert Becker, author of *The Body Electric*, tells us how living creatures can be affected by small changes in electrical currents or magnetic fields. Alarmingly, "When our species evolved, the earth's natural magnetic field had a frequency of one to twenty hertz. Today, America's electrical power delivery system, for example, has a sixty-hertz frequency. How can we sustain a three-fold increase?" Becker continues, "Electromagnetic fields have become *the* environmental health problem of the nineties." Feng shui can help us understand how to control the power of such environmental forces.

The sights we see, sounds we hear, smells we experience, and sensations of touch all mesh to comprise our experience with a physical space. In addition to our biological responses, we are creatures of culture and social conditions. The quality of experience is determined by a culture's spin. For example, the Eskimo sees hundreds of variations in snow, while native Floridians might view snow simplistically.

When I was fifteen, my family sent me to visit my uncle Willie, who lived in Madrid, Spain. He and my aunt Minnie treated me like royalty. One evening while supping in their sprawling dining room overlooking one of Madrid's splendid grand boulevards, I heard the sounds of music, generated I was told, by Los Tunas, a traditional mariachi-type band of male university students dressed in long flowing black capes who serenaded up and down the streets hoping to entice young ladies onto their balconies. When I stepped out on my aunt's balcony, I noticed other young women on other terraces waving long colorful streamers. My aunt Minnie told me that if a young woman fancied one of the troubadours, she would toss a ribbon to her favorite and he would pin this colorful silk strip onto his long black cape. Whoever collected the most ribbons was deemed the most popular. "Come with me," she said, and we both dashed inside to search for ribbons.

The next thing I knew, troubadours were pounding on my uncle's front door. All of a sudden I was closely surrounded by eight or so high-spirited university students. And the operative word was *close*! No one stood more than three inches from my nose while talking to me. As I stepped back to give myself space, they stepped forward, eating up the distance I tried to put between their faces and mine. I felt their collective breath, smelled what they had had for dinner, and felt more and more uncomfortable as the evening wore on. I should have been in heaven, a single female surrounded by so many dashing young men. Instead I spent all my time trying to maintain what I felt was an appropriate distance from them.

Only years later did I realize that what I had experienced was a cultural disparity. An appropriate social distance in the United States is from twelve inches to eighteen inches. The three- to five-inch Spanish cultural distance was much smaller than what I was accustomed to. My personal space had been invaded, and it did not feel comfortable!

Similarly, each culture has the kinds of memory clues advocated by Quintilian in ancient Rome that provide unique details to its cities and living spaces. Although the words *feng shui* are used to describe an ancient Chinese discipline, they are only a banner under which a multilayered information system is organized. An understanding of a person's relationship to place is too broad to be confined to one culture or time frame. For six thousand years, the Chinese have enriched their lives by understanding how space affects experience. Because of their historical connection, it is fitting to salute the Chinese for their pioneering efforts by retaining the name *feng shui* as the rubric under which myriad disciplines can find a home. But only when we separate the cultural anomalies from feng shui can we apply its truths universally. The subtleties of feng shui experienced through a Chinese perspective may seem delicate and finite. Like poets and monks, feng shui in its original form is both useless and indispensable. The values woven into its teachings must be extracted to reveal the central truths. Better to transform feng shui into a flexible system to ensure its survival.

Our experience of place is as integral to life as flesh is to bones. Neither can exist without being buttressed by the other. All things should be considered in determining how to have satisfying relationships, maintaining our health, and reaching maximum personal potential. With a knowledge of feng shui we are able to adjust our surroundings to drive our lives toward exquisite completeness.

Place envelops and influences all experiences. It is as silent and as vital as the air we breathe.

2

What Is Feng Shui?

The words *feng* and *shui* are Chinese for "wind" and "water," images that orbit our sentient field. The Chinese proverb "As it is above, so it will be below" suggests our interconnectedness with this sphere. Our place in this system is central to our self-actualization. We can orchestrate our fate by manipulating an environment. In many ways feng shui is a tool for our personal as well as our collective survival and growth.

Feng shui identifies conditions in a living space that affect us in either positive or negative ways. According to feng shui, the language of an environment tells a story, and if we change the elements of our surroundings, we can improve the story.

In the first few hours of life survival is determined by place. If a fertilized egg is not in the right spot in the womb, a placenta will not form. Feng shui, an ancient Chinese art of placement, is organized around the premise that *where* we are is as important as *who* we are. Throughout life, interaction with the world is impaired when our surroundings are not nourishing.

The ancient Chinese discipline of feng shui dates back at least three thousand years, although its philosophy can be traced back to teachings from six thousand years ago. Feng shui has remained honored by the Chinese population over the millennia, although in the last one hundred years feng shui has lost status. The Communist Chinese viewed it as an antiquated feudal system, and the Chinese in Hong Kong reduced its essence to helping businesses thrive. Hong Kong looked to the West for guidance for contemporary life and relegated feng shui to a more superstitious, mystical practice. The West, however, has not had the benefit of a consistent person-to-place philosophy through the ages, despite the fact that many revered historical figures have given our relationship with the environment its due. For example, Hippocrates, whose oath outlines the duties and obligations of physicians,considered environmental influences to be central to healing. In the seventeenth century an English scholar, Robert Burton, compiled *The Anatomy of Melancholy*, which referred to the relationship of climate to temperament.

Psychologist Abraham Maslow was among the first in the twentieth century to test how environment affects our opinion of others. In an ingenious experiment conducted at Brandeis University in the 1960s, he created three rooms: an ugly one, a beautiful one, and an average one. He gathered photographs of people's faces and distributed them to a team of interviewers. Each interviewer was assigned to one of the rooms. Maslow intentionally misled the interviewers about the purpose of the experiment, telling them he was researching facial characteristics in relation to personality traits. For example, were small eyes associated with untrustworthiness? The interviewers had no idea that the settings were being scrutinized.

Interviewees were asked to describe their feelings about each photograph. The results were astonishing. A face viewed in the ugly environment was described negatively, yet in the beautiful room the same photograph was assigned positive attributes. Interestingly, in the ordinary room more faces were described as people with adverse personality traits than as those with positive traits. Clearly this proves how environment affects our perception of others. (Note that universal feng shui cannot interpret what is beauty, because beauty is always filtered through culture. Although there are universal standards of beauty that are mutually accepted, taste is relevant in deciding what it is we want to live with. Therefore, feng shui acknowledges standards of beauty without dictating them in any given situation.)

I too had an intuitive hunch that environment exerted a significant impact on our lives and sought through years of schooling to find a discipline that coalesced these ideas. In fact, in the early 1970s I constructed and taught a course for an alternative high school in New Jersey entitled "Aspects of Human Space." My students read the works of anthropologist Edward T. Hall, architect Christopher Alexander, and social theorist Jane Jacobs. Searching for a discernible thread of knowledge to link person with place, I had these high school students all over the map of scholarly activity.

It was like a bolt of lightning when one day I picked up a reprint of E. J. Eitel's 1873 book on feng shui. Flashes of pulsating neon exploded in my head. I had found the discipline I sought!

Feng shui was devised through the cultural paradigms of China, where a rather stable social structure varies little from generation to generation. This, coupled with China's unique geography, flavored feng shui so that it was suitable only for this ancient culture. For example, one feng shui rule suggests that it is unlucky to have a home not in the shape of a rectangle or a square. If we try to apply this position through the framework of contemporary life, we uncover major flaws. Here's why: Most Chinese households consisted of a father, mother, offspring, and occasionally a revered elder. From town to town and house to house, few families deviated from this pattern. A unified shape for a home reflected these realities. If a room protruded form the main frame, the activity conducted in this space was outside the center or heart of the home's activities.

Today, however, we have a great variety of family configurations. A burgeoning number of people work at home. While proximity to family life is beneficial in many ways, it is sometimes advantageous to have a work space separated form the hustle and bustle of everyday home life. An appendage to a rectangle or square can be an ideal location for a work space.

Both my husband I work at home. When we added on to our house, we purposely constructed two work spaces that connect to the main frame like wings on a bird. Free from distractions of family life and each other, we sit at our desks each day, tackling the tasks at hand. Moreover, when we finish work we can return to a space that has no visual connection to our workplace. We don't have to pass desks stacked with papers crying out for attention. We can relax and enjoy being home.

So, for all its validity, feng shui's belief system is not acceptable to other cultures unless its essence is extracted from its guidelines. Feng shui must be synthesized with other bodies of knowledge to meet the specific requirements of culture, geography, climate, and human uniqueness. When that is done, feng shui becomes an old friend. Toward that end, *Feng Shui: The Book of Cures* simplifies methods for identifying negative conditions in your life and then changing them to positive.

Keep in mind, though, that feng shui rules cannot be applied like a bandage. Feng shui is not a pill to ingest. *Knowledge of person* is an integral part of utilizing feng shui's advice. Personality, age, and preferences must be taken into account when interpreting feng shui's directives. *Knowledge of a culture or subculture* also determines many factors in an environment. The living spaces of an egalitarian Scandinavian family are vastly different from those of a patriarchal South American family living in upper-class splendor. *Knowledge of climate* serves as another element in the decision-making process. Decks or porches in southern climates will be used more frequently as gathering rooms than those in northern locales. I have often asked myself why terraces in newly built condominiums seem to be the same width no matter where they are built.

Take the same approach to feng shui as to dressing. Most of us know what looks good on us and what to avoid. We select clothes to fit our image, age, and body proportions. In the same way, use the feng shui rules to accommodate the specifies of your own life.

Let this book be a guide to understanding and implementing the best environmental conditions for your life. Know that the heart of feng shui is how to create living and working spaces that can add immeasurably to life's satisfactions.

3

Schools of Feng Shui

The ideas inherent in feng shui emerged from the needs of humans to codify information about the world surrounding them. Different schools of feng shui developed and relied on different tools for interpreting the notion that person and place were connected in profound ways.

There are two traditional schools of feng shui. One is the form school, which bases its findings on interpreting the shapes of objects in the physical world, and the other is the compass school, which analyzes spaces based on a magnetic needle centered within circles representing up to thirty-six different categories.

The pyramid school, which is the focus of this book, is a newer school of feng shui, one that acknowledges the universality of feng shui's concepts and adds to these by including contemporary findings in the fields of biology, psychology, architecture, and city planning.

The Form School

Most of our conscious intake in life comes from observing. We use our eyes more than any of our other senses to discern the world around us. The form school of feng shui uses the visual sense to detect shapes, colors, and textures and then interprets their meaning for the human condition.

The form school looks at certain aspects of the world and finds either positive or negative interpretations in them for those who live viewing these forms. A mountain, for example, can be either menacing or protective, depending on its visual interpretation. According to the form school, a mountain whose linear topography appears dragonlike is positive, because the ancient Chinese believed dragons augured good fortune.

The Compass School

The compass school of feng shui is not in great use today. It selects the best living spaces based on calculations from a magnetic needle that revolves around a disk. The disk differs from a traditional compass in that it has up to thirty-six concentric circles depicting different aspects of information that are dependent on this fixed reading. In the contemporary world a compass reading is more often than not inaccurate because our buildings are filled with metals that distort the readings. Whether the objects are visible such as appliances, furniture, or picture frames or hidden like our wiring, building studs, or nails, our homes are crammed with metal. As a consequence we are unlikely to capture a true compass reading.

The Pyramid School

A form school devotee will select a dragon-shaped mountain as an auspicious site just because it is dragon-shaped. A follower of the pyramid school might chose the same location but would explain the choice this way: A dragon-shaped mountain rolls gently toward a valley rather than having sharp lines that descend vertically. A mountain with a moderate slope will not spin water violently onto a valley floor. It also offers easier access to human beings. A home sited near or on a gently sloping mountain is far easier to live in than a home on its steep counterpart. The pyramid school says it is auspicious to site a home on a mountain shaped in such a way whether you see a dragon in its silhouette or not.

This interpretation of mountains is an example of how the pyramid school moves beyond ancient feng shui by interpreting concepts through a contemporary western point of view. We are an aggregate of influences external and internal. The union of elements that constitute individuality comprises the underpinnings of biological considerations, genetic configuration, and specifics of family, community, state, country, and religion. Each fosters propensities that must be honored. Eliminating one part of the human jigsaw puzzle would render the scene incomplete. Feng shui is untenable when not allowed to filter through all the segments. The pyramid school takes into account all the segments by acknowledging that we are living with different cultural, social, and, in some places, climatic conditions from the Chinese.

It is in our best interest to discern the nuances of our particular culture and social conditions so that we can implement a spirit of change to resonate with our lives, attitudes, and customs. For example, traditional Chinese feng shui considers some numbers lucky and others unlucky. Some of these notions are based on how the word sounds in Chinese. The Chinese word for the number four sounds like the word *death*, so four is unlucky in Chinese. But the word for four does not sound like *death* in English. Therefore, for us to consider number four unlucky, based on its Chinese tone, seems unreasonable.

Similarly, while ancient feng shui suggests that a master bedroom be situated at the back of a home, the pyramid school considers the configuration of the family to be of primary importance when positioning any room, architectural detail, or furniture. There is no generic best. *Best* takes into consideration specifics of culture, climate, and social conditions.

A family with children may not be best served by having the master bedroom at the back if that means separating it from the children's rooms or placing the children's rooms closer to the front door. Separation can only foster a feeling of disassociation, and the master bedroom needs to be in a position to allow the parents to fulfill their role as protectors.

On the other hand, a family without children can sometimes be best served if bedrooms are separated from the heart of the house. Whether as a guest room, an office, or a library, their successful use is often augmented by the separation.

Blending the diverse aspects of lifestyle, culture, and social conditions is the governing theme of the pyramid school. Using a partitioned pyramid to represent the different parts of the whole, the hierarchy of importance starts at the bottom, the foundation of life. Each layer depends on those underneath to sustain its existence.

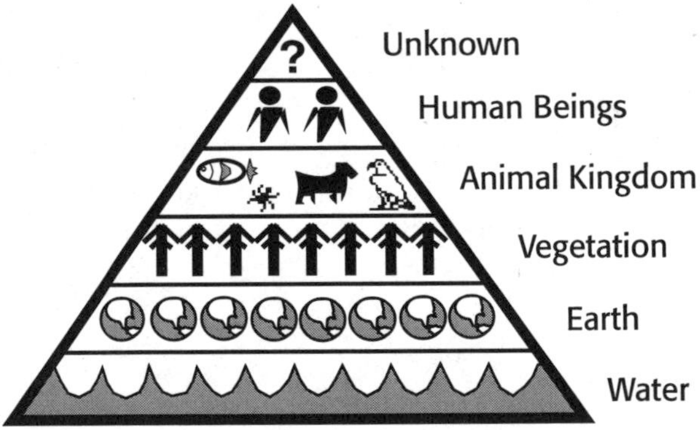

The pyramid of life

Water

Just as a fertilized egg germinates in amniotic fluid, life was born from a primordial ooze whose properties are similar to water. Even if we have all the necessary ingredients, we cannot make soup unless we have a liquid that can absorb and merge the contents. Water is a vessel that processes the mix of live forces. It is the base from which life emerges. Its properties are the elixir that gives birth to the variety of forms of life within our planet.

Earth

The earth contains us. It is a shell that holds all the parts. Like our home, it provides us with boundaries that protect us.

Vegetation

Most vegetation does not consume itself or others to thrive. Utilizing the vitality of earth and water, vegetation sustains existence through true nonviolence. Even weeds do not consume in the same way as we do, they overwhelm rather than kill intentionally.

Animal Kingdom

The animal kingdom is more complex. Animals need to feed on other species to survive, eating either plants or other animals. When the dynamics between supply of resources and use become tipped to overuse, both species decline.

Human Beings

Atop the identifiable pyramid sits the human species. Unique as a species, we have the potential to impact in a way no other earthly feature or creature has. Exhibiting a lack of sensitivity to the plight of our supporters, humans have depleted and destroyed resources necessary for survival. In comparison with our importance in the scheme of life, we have weighted our place in the system to exceed an appropriate portion.

As a minuscule dispensable part of the whole, we might consider our place on this earth a gift, one to be cherished and nurtured. By guiding our passion and intensity for personal happiness to include benefits for the whole, we will be rewarded in unforeseen ways. We can best thrive by understanding the nuances between enough and excess.

Unknown

It would be naive to consider our knowledge complete. We have seen the science and philosophy in one era topple like building blocks on a child's toy tower. As a discipline, the pyramid school strives to stay contemporary and consolidate the knowledge of change under the umbrella of feng shui. City planners, architects, landscape designers, interior designers, psychologists, and biologists have helped solidify input from many disciplines into a viable body of knowledge that will allow us to thrive in our place on this earth without compromising the integrity and well-being of the whole.

This book has chosen the pyramid school as the perspective through which to interpret feng shui. The pyramid school seeks to reveal the erudition behind intuition, to lay the groundwork for understanding by exploring the whys behind each ancient dictate. When we understand what makes a specific situation inauspicious, then we are likely to implement cures through the suggestions in this book or invoke them by imagination. The destination is more important than the route, for the goal is fixed while a route is selected.

4

The Ingredients of Feng Shui

Feng shui rests its interpretation upon three philosophical principles. The notions of Tao, yin/yang, and chi are enmeshed into Chinese culture not unlike the way in which life, liberty, and the pursuit of happiness are integral to our culture.

Tao—To Be Connected

Like the chain of DNA linking characteristics together to form a human being, the Tao is the means to the end. *Tao* can be translated as "the way." Like a canary in a coal mine, diseased vegetation often augurs human disintegration. We are connected to the entire system of life, and our lives cannot be separated from the life forces around us. Even when we cannot see it, each part of life depends on another to create a whole. When one part is crushed, the entire unit comes to a halt. To be unconnected impairs our lives.

How can Taoism be applied to a home? One way would be to re-create shapes and experiences from outside. Do you have any plants, paintings of landscapes, or even colors similar to those outside your home? Does your home have a sense of connectedness from floor to floor or room to room? Color, style of furniture, or type of artwork can be the thread linking each individual part in a home.

On a recent consultation I observed a disparity between members of a family. The parents were focused people who traveled many spiritual paths such as meditating, eating wholesome foods, avoiding mind-altering drugs, and staying physically active. Throughout their home this was visible in photos of marathon runs and from their exotic travels and in a room they had furnished exclusively as a refuge for meditation.

Their son's room was a glaring exception. Except for pictures of marijuana plants, the room had little to distinguish it from a motel room. There was nothing that identified his "self" or what he liked other than this solitary weed. How a child's room connects emotionally, visually, and philosophically to a parent's point of view is a part of Tao's considerations. His room was a red flag that he was separating himself from his parents.

When nature, people, and their preferences are sequestered in an exclusive area and not shared by the whole, trouble might be brewing. How the threads of each family member's life weave into the big picture is a crucial element in the Tao of a home.

City dwellers rarely have a great deal of visual connection with nature. Still, it's possible for those who live with a human-made landscape to thrive. Do you like what you see? Is the altered environment satisfying? Do you feel nurtured by the view? Does your view include a thriving street filled with prosperous shops and restaurants or are you cloistered from street life by viewing an air shaft between two buildings?

To be in the Tao is to be connected. Whether your home is rural, suburban, or urban, to feel deeply at peace you should feel positively enmeshed with your surroundings.

Yin/Yang—To Find the Balance

Yin and yang represent opposites, like high/low, big/little, hot/cold. Unlike our Western adversarial notion of opposites, however, they are complementary.

Consider a yo-yo. This toy functions by utilizing two extremes in a harmonious relationship with each other. Without each extreme, a yo-yo could not work. It needs the "up" as much as the "down." Yin and yang always need each other to balance a game, room, or life.

Yin	Yang
dark colors	light colors
muted colors	bright colors
curved lines (furniture)	straight lines (most office equipment)
dim lighting	bright lighting
moist (basements)	dry (attics)
low (sofas)	high (breakfronts)
quiet (most bathrooms)	loud (rooms near busy roads, kitchens)
soft cushions	wood benches
stair treads	stair risers
empty walls	filled bookshelves
decreases (dimmer switches)	grows (plants)
hides (closets, recessed lighting)	obvious (dining room table)
earthy (seated furniture)	urbane (desks)
cool (windows, fans)	warm (ovens, heating vents)
still (chairs)	active (fans, desk chairs with casters)
odors (mold)	fragrances (candles, cooking)

A yin personality is reflective, introspective, quiet, and down to earth, while a yang person is outgoing and talkative, loves sports, and jumps out of bed before the alarm clock stops ringing. However, even a quiet person needs to be social, just as a social butterfly needs some quiet time. A person without balance often ends up breaking down mentally or physically.

The previous page shows a list of yin and yang characteristics as defined by the ancients, with examples of how they could apply to a home or office.

Remembering what is yin or yang matters less than paying attention to where each condition falls on a continuum. Extremes can be tolerated for only a short period of time. Being in solitary confinement or in the middle of a mass rally are both intolerable as frequent life experiences. So, when you're examining your home, see if any area is weighted in one direction. If it is, determine if the energy being evoked by the imbalance feels appropriate for you. To motivate you to do, create, and translate thoughts into actions, your office might need more yang (active energy) than yin (passive energy). On the

TO ADD YIN

1. Use less light (reduce lightbulb wattage).
2. Use seating with low backs or furniture that is less than half the room's height.
3. Use muted or dark colors (burgundy rather than fire-engine red).
4. Add fountains with aerating waters.
5. Use furniture or fabric patterns with curved lines.
6. Use fabrics that feel soft, silky, or velvety.
7. Add peacefulness (turn off the radio or TV).
8. Turn off ceiling fans or ducts that blow air.
9. Be alone.

other hand, a bedroom is a perfect example of a room that can be weighted toward a feeling of yin. There we need to feel cozy, nurtured, and enveloped in stability and stillness.

If you find the imbalance inappropriate in a particular room, add whichever element is lacking.

Here's one example of how to adjust conditions in a room to feel more comfortable and be attuned to your needs: If a bedroom is filled with too much yang, change the lightbulbs to a lesser wattage, toss a muted shawl over a computer, or block a window by placing a plant in front.

On the other hand, if you feel unmotivated, listless, and tired, consider adding yang to your office, kitchen, or hobby room. In those cases adding light, bright colors, and music or hanging the tools of your trade on the walls nearby could provide the inspiration you need.

To Add Yang

1. Make lights brighter.
2. Use tall furniture like high-backed chairs.
3. Add bright colors.
4. Use a dehumidifier to dry the atmosphere.
5. Use solid fabrics or fabrics with vertical stripes.
6. Add action through movement and sound like ticking clocks or tabletop toys.
7. Turn on fans or open a window to allow in a breeze.
8. Display collections of books, accessories, or art.
9. Invite company over.

CHI—VITALITY

I laughed when I looked up the word *vitality* in the dictionary and found the definition "the peculiarity of distinguishing the living from the nonliving." Chi is vitality. All spaces are containers for life and need chi, but the amount needed depends on a room's function. Without chi there is nothing. With too much chi there is chaos. Chi should move through a home effortlessly, freely, and with dignity. It should never get stuck or trapped. If a path leading to a room's main function or other areas of a home is blocked, then your task is to remove the obstacle. If you have to squeeze by furniture to get into or out of a seating grouping, then your task is to liberate the chi by moving some furniture out of the way.

More often than not we are attracted to chi qualities in people, places, and things. Not long ago, hoping to pique a female friend's interest in meeting a male friend, I found myself using only chi descriptions. I told her he was funny and bright, played tennis, and flew a plane. She seemed interested. I probably could not have interested her in him had I told her his favorite color was green, he wore T-shirts with collars, or he read the *Miami Herald*.

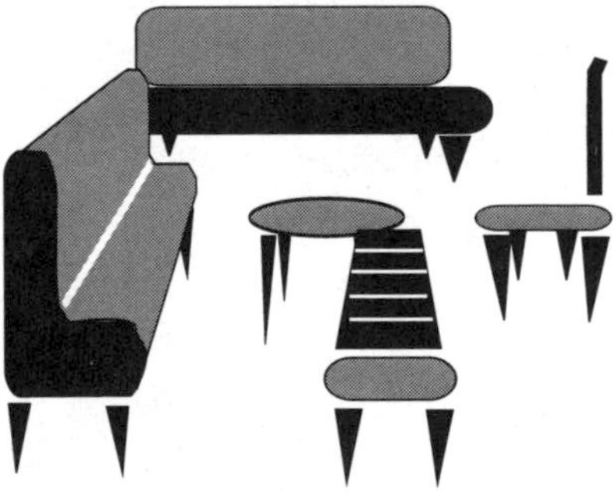

Chi cannot move freely when furniture is too close together in a seating grouping.

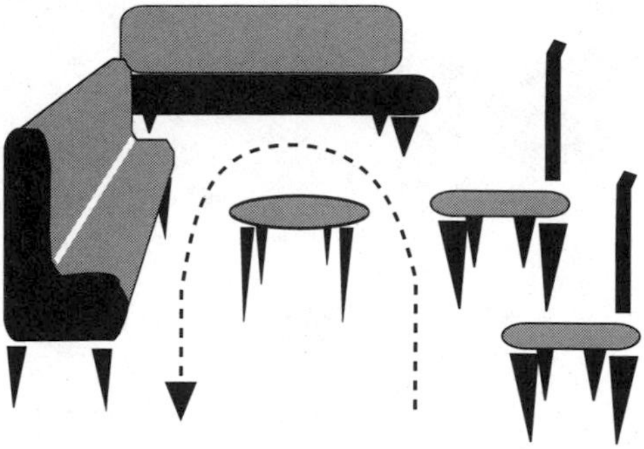

The solution is to move a piece of furniture to allow people and chi to move in and out freely.

Chi does not move in mysterious ways. It pulls us in certain directions and commands attention. To identify chi, just look at where you are compelled to move and what you see first in any space. Like blood flowing through a body, chi is the path through living spaces. Give chi adequate space to sweep you into the main areas in a home, and you will be rewarded by feeling energized, upbeat, and positive. Facing a wall when entering a home can stop chi, while a staircase directly opposite a front door can sweep you away from the main living space.

You can evaluate the flow of chi for a whole home or for a corner of a room. The pathways through an entire house, the focus of a room, or how individual artifacts are arranged on a table can determine the chi of that specific area. Consider how an empty cocktail table in front of a sofa can change when a few objects are placed there. It shifts from being overlooked to being engaging.

From an entire household to a pattern on a plate, chi is the one attribute that can alter any essence. Where chi leads, you will follow.

Following is a list of conditions that can either carry forward or inhibit the flow of chi in a home.

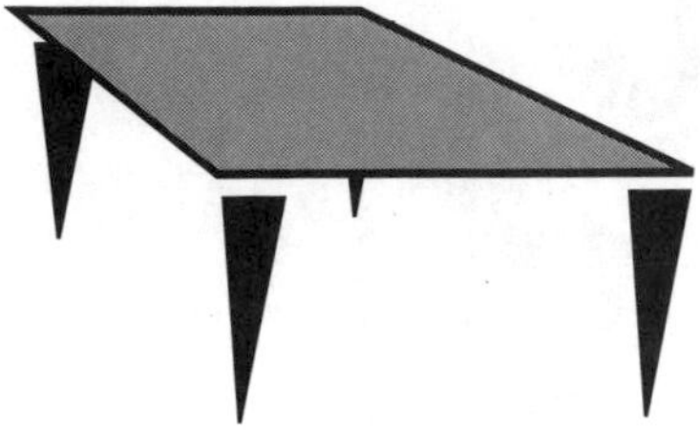

An unadorned table is usually overlooked; a table decorated with objects draws attention.

CHI ENHANCING	CHI INHIBITING
pathways	walls
windows	closed doors
open space	clutter
light	dark
thermal comfort	too hot or too cold
circles and undulating lines	corners, triangles
wind-sensitive objects	lack of movement

5

The Five Elements

Before science and logic formed the prescription for a culture's identity, humans relied on common sense, intuition, and observation for answers to questions. Even with today's research, logic, and explanations available to justify our beliefs, we must rely to some extent on trust. In most cases we recognize truth when it is held up to the light even if no scientific backing yet exists. In the same way, all human beings perceive the five elements. Fire, earth, metal, water, and wood are so integrated into our knowing that few words are needed to explain how we feel about them.

The five elements are the main ingredients in the soup of feng shui, and they must be mixed in a particular way, or the results won't be delectable. A loaf of bread would be hard as a tack instead of fluffy and light if yeast were added at the wrong moment. Timing and proportion are essential.

If you think about how you experience each element, you'll realize that its essence strikes a commonsense chord. Fire, for example, is dynamic. Flames leap, consume, and charge the atmosphere with warmth. How fire combines positively or negatively with the other elements and how these relationships apply in your home or office are also matters of common sense.

A stove is obviously a fire element in our homes. A refrigerator cools by manipulation of the element water.

Placing a stove (fire) next to a refrigerator (water) jars us unconsciously much like a fingernail scratching a blackboard because water puts out fire. It is, therefore, best to separate a stove from a refrigerator or a fire element from a water element.

Fire also produces earth in the form of ashes. Moreover, earth cannot be consumed or ignited. Therefore, placing a fire element next to an earth element is positive. A brick, stone, or tile fireplace surround feels right in part because fire and earth are in a positive relationship to each other.

Finally, there are times when we will want to increase or reduce the experiential properties of an element. On a frigid winter's day we feel warmer when a fire element is augmented through color (red) or line (triangular). By upholstering a chair in a thick red flamestitch fabric rather than a lightweight blue gauzy one we are augmenting the fire element.

Positive Relationships of the Elements

The basis of a positive relationship lies in one element's ability to assist in the creation or release of the other.

1. Fire to earth: The remains of fire produce earth.
2. Earth to metal: Within the earth are the components that blend to create the metals.
3. Metal to water: This relationship can be compared to a positive parent-child association. Parents provide the strong container in which a child flourishes. Their role is not unlike metal—immutable, strong, and undaunted. However, parents must allow children to evolve into adults and leave the nest. We don't dump a child on a doorstep to face the adult world as if we're pitching a bucket of water out a front door. Just as

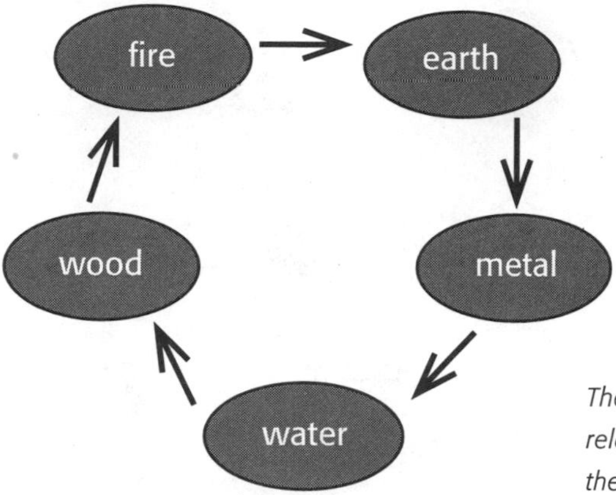

The positive relationships of the elements

water bleeds to the outside of metal through condensation, growing up comes in small increments, drop by drop, until children have evolved into adults.

4. Water to wood: Water is the staff of life for wood.
5. Wood to fire: Wood provides fuel for fire.

Negative Relationships of the Elements

Reversing the direction produces a negative relationship.

1. Fire to wood: Fire consumes wood.
2. Wood to water: Wood absorbs water.
3. Water to metal: Water can corrode metal.
4. Metal to earth: Metal absorbs earth to produce itself.
5. Earth to fire: Earth can squelch fire.

Neutral or Negative Relationships of the Elements

Finally, the elements across from each other can be neutral or negative.

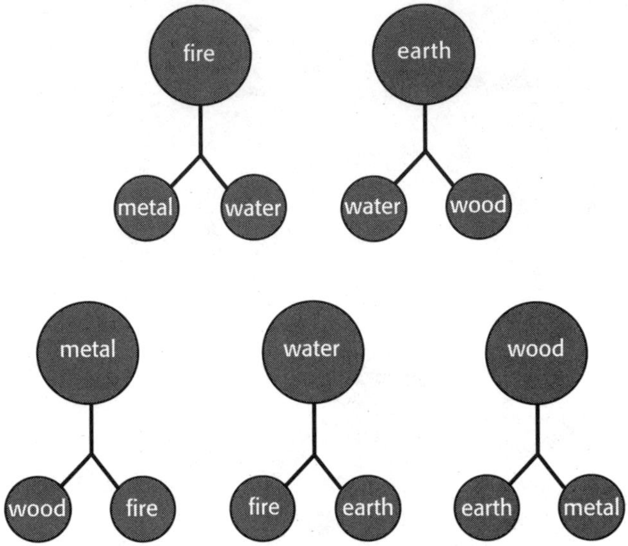

The neutral or negative relationships of the elements

Fire to Metal or Water

1. Fire to metal: Metal conducts heat quickly and can become hot to the touch. Metal also conducts cold quickly and can deter a feeling of warmth in cases when the fire element needs to be augmented.
2. Fire to water: Water can save a burning home but can also stamp out a lifesaving campfire.

Earth to Water or Wood

1. Earth to water: Just as a river can move masses of land to secure its course, water can erode earth.
2. Earth to wood: Earth supplies nutrients to wood to grow but by doing so depletes itself slowly but surely unless replenished.

Metal to Wood or Fire

1. Metal to wood: Metal is a stronger material than wood and, when pitted against wood, like a gun against a bow and arrow, wins. Metal in the form of an ax can be life sustaining when it helps to fell a tree.
2. Metal to fire: Fire heats metal and can make metal uncomfortable to touch or can allow metal to radiate heat on a frigid winter day.

Water to Fire or Earth

1. Water to fire: Water can extinguish fire.
2. Water to earth: Earth can overwhelm water. We dump mounds of earth to fill swamps to gain land mass. While earth may temporarily overcome water, like a jetty built to prevent shoreline erosion, time will reverse its effect and water will triumph.

Wood to Earth or Metal

1. Wood to earth: Wood consumes the nutrients of the earth but the two can produce a healthy tree to provide shade or building material.
2. Wood to metal: Wood can be mismatched when used in combination with metal. Moisture or dryness does little to change the shape of metal, while wood expands and contracts easily. A metal frame can separate from a wood base because the reactions of metal and wood are not in sync.

The five elements can be represented by color, shape, material, use, direction, and emotion as well as their direct source. When a situation needs adjusting, one way to effect change is to add the color, shape, material, or emotion that each element expresses. When you are down in the dumps, add fire to a setting. When you are nervous about a pending examination, add water to a setting. When you need to be courageous, add wood. When you need razor-sharp mental ability, add metal. Here's how to do it.

FIRE CAN BE EXPRESSED BY . . .

Color: Red, the color of a flame. Energizing, engaging, and compelling.

Shape: Triangle, the shape of a flame. Dynamic and volatile, as in a love triangle or the Bermuda triangle.

Material: Although fire is hardly an appropriate material for a building or furnishing, a pattern of a material can express this element. Tiles laid in a chevron pattern, fabric with a flamestitch design, or napkins folded into a triangle shape all engage the feeling of fire.

Use: To warm internally or externally. While an oven warms food, a napkin folded in a triangle starts the digestive juices flowing through its dynamic shape.

Direction: South, toward warmth and the sun, is the direction of fire in the Northern Hemisphere.

Emotion: To incite or initiate. Energy needed for intellectual, emotional, or spiritual pursuits is augmented by fire. Fire is often used in ceremonies to commence important events. Carrying the flame at the Olympic games, meditating before a candle, and adorning a dining table with candles all invoke a sense of opening oneself up to an experience, be it athletic achievement, spiritual awakening, or receptivity to nourishment. Fire in an emotional sense does not still the heart but rather sears it apart to receive.

Earth Can Be Expressed By . . .

Color: Primary colors are as basic to life as the elements of earth, fire, and water. Because fire and water are associated with red and blue, respectively, and because the earth is a fusion of tones that are filled with hues of the colors yellow, terra cotta, and brown, it seems fitting that the earth be associated with these colors.

Shape: Square represents the spirit of earth, since we view the earth as a container for human life. Our basically straight physical form requires mostly uninterrupted lines; we cannot comfortably sit or sleep on a curved surface. As our home, the earth is designed to protect us and make us feel secure; straight equal lines feel stable and firm. A low square home, a square room, a squat chair, a short sofa, and a square table are earth shapes.

Material: Clay, brick, mud, and cement.

Use: Any object that adds stability, boundaries, and unification can promote a feeling of the earth element. A low square coffee table, a double bed, trays, computer and TV screens, and the wells underneath a stove's burners can add stability, boundaries, and unification to the territory they dominate.

Direction: The earth is associated with a center. We are centered in ourselves; therefore, the earth represents self.

Emotion: We feel peaceful and secure when we are near earth's elements. Earth attaches and roots us in place and is a compelling material to add in an environment.

METAL CAN BE EXPRESSED BY . . .

Color: White, the absence of color, reflects whatever surrounds it. Metal, because of its potential to be shiny, is like white insofar as it mirrors or reflects. The colors of steel gray, copper, silver, and gold can reflect the emotional properties of metal because they actually are the colors of different alloys.

Shape: Round. Metal will bubble into round beads as it is heated by a welder's torch. The bubbling molecules will blend with those of the welding rod. If heat continues to be applied after that point, the metal vaporizes. Therefore, when metal becomes round it is at a critical point. It will either blend with another metal and become stronger or disintegrate.

Material: Many earth materials have metal as a component, since earth contains the ingredients for metal. Computers, TVs, refrigerators, radios, clocks, and concealed items like electrical wiring, framing studs, and nails contain the attributes of metal.

Use: Metal can be represented by curved architectural details, pathways, and furniture or by round windows, seating groups, tables, doorknobs, cabinet and drawer handles, and dishes. Steel gray, copper, and gold can be represented in fabric, paint, and stain.

Direction: West. We gain the strength of metal by building on our experiences. Since the sun sets in the west, this direction can be associated with the potency of the aggregate of experience.

Emotion: Discernment, control, and deep sorrow. Metal has many divergent personalities. Many cultures, including ours, have assigned a certain status to some metals. Adornment in gold and silver, for example, implies a lifestyle purged of the mundane. On the other hand, metal is often used to restrain. Prison bars, handcuffs, and metal stays in bras are used to control us.

The drama of metal's transformation from a solid into a gas through extreme temperatures parallels life's intensity. Grief is the result of extremes like metal's fiery mutation.

Water Can Be Expressed By . . .

Color: Blue and black are the colors of water, for light is absorbed by large volumes of water.

Shape: Like waves during a storm, the water shape is mercurial. Undulating lines best represent this element.

Material: Glass, like water, is fluid. If a piece of glass stands on its side, over time it will become thicker at the bottom. The molecules at the top will flow toward the bottom. Like water, glass can be transparent and can block but not necessarily shield. The sun's rays penetrate glass and water, but the wind's momentum is blocked.

Use: A room with glass tables, sinks, toilets, tubs, fountains, and fish tanks or many windows evokes the water element. A serrated knife, a free-flowing line in a pattern, confetti, or a garden hose tossed across a lawn all can assume the properties of water.

Direction: As we go down into a cave or body of water or go up into space, all things become darker and colder. North, the direction of cold in our hemisphere and prolonged days of darkness, represents the element water.

Emotion: Water can by nonaction consume. By its volume alone it can wear away stone mountains; by its proximity it can rust metal to dust and rot wood to disintegration. When a stream of water encounters an obstacle, it yields and finds another path. We can become open to experience and understanding by acting like water and yielding. Water can give us peace of mind and a feeling of oneness, for it ultimately connects all living things. When we are as one with the current we can find true contentment.

WOOD CAN BE EXPRESSED BY . . .

Color: Green represents life, growth, and health. The green of a tree's leaf is a sign of its vitality. A dormant or lifeless tree does not express a bright color.

Shape: Rectangle. The silhouette of a tree expresses growth. As it matures, a tree's trunk soars into a larger and larger rectangle.

Material: Wood, cardboard, paper, and composite products made with wood, like particleboard, plasterboard, doors, and certain roof tiles.

Use: Many of our building materials and furniture are made of wood products. In fact, it is odd to be in temperate-climate housing that has not used wood in some form. Environments that don't support the growth of wood are often hostile to human habitation.

Household items such as chairs, cabinets, headboards, cutting boards, knife handles, pencils, banisters, picture frames, decorative boxes, and lamps are typical uses of wood.

Direction: Beginnings herald the promise of growth and change, the kind of growth and change manifested by a tree. Since the sunrise is the beginning of each new day, east is wood's direction.

Emotion: Wood, as the Goliath of vegetation, conveys desire for transformation, growth, and change. Its permutations are evidenced by visible yearly changes. Successful change inspires us to hope, risk, and adventure. Wood gathers strength through what is obvious and what is hidden. With its capacity to expand under pressure, wood inspires us to grow even though the change may not be easy. It is both a leader and a follower, for while it surges toward the light, wood can bend to circumvent whatever is in the way.

How to Reduce or Augment the Five Elements in a Room

While we cannot always impersonate nature, the rhythms of our life should model its wisdom. For example, we do not have twenty-four hours of sunlight each day, in part because living creatures would not thrive without a time for inactivity. In our environments, having bright light for approximately one half of a day can provide proper energy and support optimum human functioning. A room's energy should be consistent with its intended use.

It is in my best interest to have my writing room filled with energy that inspires me to create. Through color alone I have supported the best proportions of the five elements to suit my needs. I have added appropriate amounts of fire, earth, metal, water, and wood with colors to nurture, energize, and infuse me with stamina while I write. To light my mental fires, I have splashed vibrant reds throughout this room. A red wall clock; purple, red, and black spiral tile flooring, and a red telephone ignite my aptitude. A verdigris table base, green striped curtains, and two wide rectangular green wall stripes support the birth of ideas and books. A black desk fortifies the persistence I need for the job because water always gets where it needs to. White walls and writing paper provide a clear background for intellectual pursuits and are the tabula rasa on which I can construct my thoughts. Outside a sliding glass door is an herb garden on a red roof. Pots filled with earth support

TYPICAL PROBLEMS	CURES THROUGH THE ADDITION OF THE FIVE ELEMENTS
too much noise or activity	add water element
need to transmit ideas	add water
need to relax	add earth and water
need to feel grounded	add earth
need to quell fears	add earth
too quiet or sluggish	add fire
need to feel inspired	add fire
need to think	add fire, wood, and metal
need to break out of your shell	add wood
need to feel happier	add wood
need to communicate	add metal
need to be cultured	add metal

my mini-garden, which replenishes my soul as I search for ways to express my thoughts. I am very content to spend ten to twelve hours a day in this room.

Introduce the complementary element if a space is out of balance, or reduce an element that overwhelms a space. For example, a hyperactive child in a room filled with the fire element, an element that excites and stimulates, needs water to calm him, while an insecure child in the same room would find the energy intimidating and would need earth to assist with a feeling of connectedness and stability.

If you are feeling out of sync in a room and don't know why, see if there is too much or too little of one element. For example, I could reduce the water element represented by black, several free-form patterns, and large glass windows by adding more fire or adjust the concept of water by introducing wood. Which of these choices is best should be determined by experimenting.

6

The Pyramid School's Ba-Gua: The Effect of Different Parts of a Room

We learn to use different parts of our bodies to express different emotions and intentions. But did you know that different parts of a room define different areas of our lives? The Chinese have identified the parts of a room where specific human experiences thrive. The success or failure of those parts of life when carried out in that room depend on how the room is shaped and what kind of furniture and accessories are placed there.

We rarely give a second thought to how different parts of our bodies are used to express different emotions. While there is a biological basis for why we use our arms to embrace, for example, it is our culture that determines the attributes of a kiss. Traditional feng shui uses a ba-gua, or an octagon shape, to identify the optimum locations for different activities. There are eight sections to a ba-gua, and each section is assigned a feature. The pyramid school modifies the ancient ba-gua areas so they are in sync with contemporary Western culture as well as biology.

Ba-gua is based on the idea that right and left have inherent meaning for human beings, just as the right and left hemispheres of the brain control different functions. The right side of the brain controls emotion and

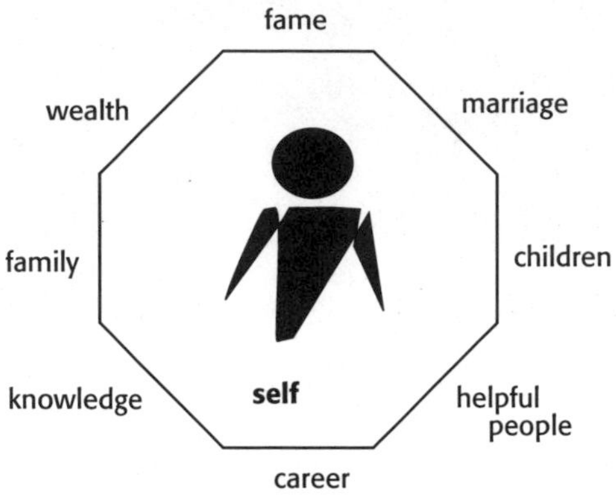

Old ba-gua

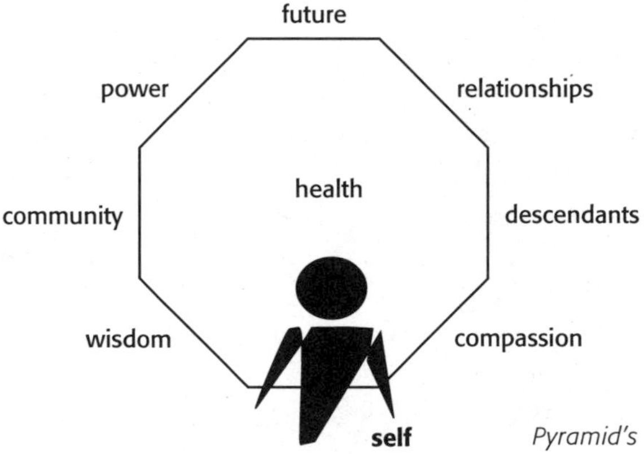

Pyramid's ba-gua

abstract thinking, while the left side handles the practical aspects of cognition. Artists use their right side to create, accountants their left side to compute. Thus, it is natural to align areas relevant to our emotional life on the right side of a room and areas delegated to critical thinking on the left. In the concept of ba-gua everything is relative to the entry into the room, so *left* means what is on your left as you enter, *right* what you can see on the right from the doorway.

Since most of the world is right-handed, the right hand is often used to express friendship and greeting,

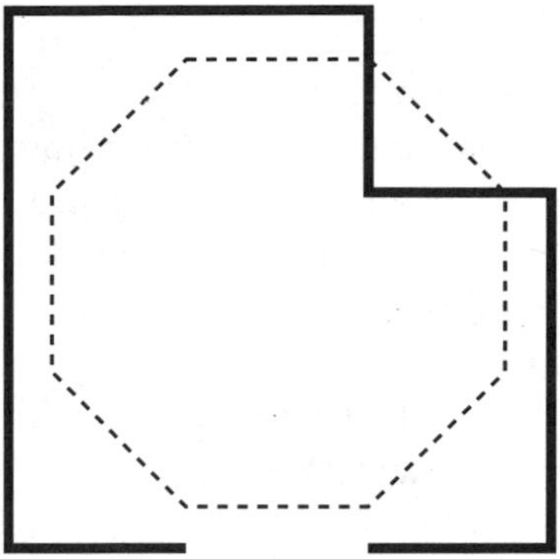

Missing relationship corner. If a couple's bedroom is missing this corner, we could anticipate a strained relationship.

as in shaking hands. Consequently the right side of a room should have a closer connection to emotions. Relationships, descendants, and compassion fit neatly with our emotional life.

The left side of a room should be devoted to organized, logical brain activities. Accomplishing something left-handed requires more concentration and effort for most people, as do wisdom, community, and power.

In the center, like a pinwheel's anchor, is health. When we feel secure and strong, all things seem achievable. Like a tetherball flying through the air, the self can take off when rotating around a thriving center.

Center: Health

Have you ever walked into a waiting room with all the seating backed up against the walls? Such rooms usually feel heartless because the center is void. Until recently Westerners tended to place furnishings around the perimeter of rooms in homes as well. Only dining room tables, beds, and thrones were likely to be arranged in the center. Yet offices with desks flat against a wall rather than perpendicular to it usually feel less grounded to those who work there.

In Eastern cultures furniture is more often found in the physical center of a room instead of around the edges. That is because feng shui instructs that a home or room without a center is like a body without a heart. What keeps a family or work group from floating off in its own orbit is the gravity exerted by the space's center.

In the traditional ba-gua the center is occupied by the self; the pyramid school translates that as health. Both self and health could be said to be the center of our lives—without physical and emotional peace we get grumpy, unhappy, and stressed out. For that reason the center of any room or home should reflect health.

First make sure the heart of each room supports the activity of the place. Keep in mind that the heart does not have to be the exact center, as long as the eyes converge on this area of importance when people first enter the room. Then be sure the center of the space has organization and a clear or uncomplicated vista to help propel the occupants toward life-sustaining activities. Clutter and disorganization in a room encourage frenetic and chaotic lives.

FUTURE

The future is most often expressed as a physical distance, as in wishing on a star, so the spot farthest from the door in a room should symbolically spur the occupants toward future conquests. One way to do so is by honoring the past, perhaps with a family portrait, a trophy, a pair of treasured skates, or something else to connect people to past accomplishments.

Acquire a physical representation for a future goal. A teenager might use a basketball or a pair of dancing slippers to represent a goal, while a business owner might position a poster with sales goals measuring potential future business growth in future's area. Whatever you dare to dream, place in this faraway spot.

Relationships

Although we still need meaningful, intimate connections with others, we no longer censure deviations from traditional families. Many seek to secure the benefits of a partnership without being confined to a traditional marriage, so traditional feng shui's marriage area is pyramid's relationship area. Relationships attempt to satisfy a need to be happy and peaceful. Like a hand extended in a greeting, the far right-hand side of a room best represents a focus for relationships.

We can support that section of a room by providing space for two persons to communicate. Placing two chairs and a table there is an obvious choice. Highlight the location. Enhance it with a circle of light, favorite colors, and chi-enhancing objects like plants, movement-sensitive objects, or light-refracting items like mirrors. Augment a sense of being grounded with items made of wood or earth. The sound or sight of water via fountain, fish tank, or bowl filled with water and fresh flowers is another way to adorn this dominion. If space doesn't permit much, simply hang a picture with two symbols (two people, two boats, two flowers, two strokes of bold red).

Descendants

Tangential to our personal needs is the desire for our lives to have some meaning after we are no longer here. Science postulates that the basis for a primate's feeling of love for its offspring lies in a need to replicate its genetic pool. Since dependency on adults lasts longer in humans than any other species on earth, humans needed a trait that would secure the desire to care for immature offspring for an extended period of time. Our deep emotional connection to our progeny is, in part, our species' adaptation to a need to provide long-term care.

We live in a crowded world. Specific biological changes that occur because of crowding have been documented by the work of Edward Hall. His experiments with rodents revealed how a species suffers physically and psychologically when a certain number is exceeded. Hall discovered that aberrant behavior, fewer offspring, and enlarged adrenal glands, leading to an increase in disease, were the consequences of crowding. Even if smaller and smaller numbers of people reproduce, a human's need to impact on future generations does not subside. Whether we have children or not, it is a natural human desire to be connected to the future. For those who have not reproduced, descendants might include nieces, nephews, neighbors' children, or other children in a working or community environment.

In my writing room I happen to have a closet in the descendants section. Since knowledge is my gift to my biological as well as spiritual descendants, I keep a box of my favorite books in this closet. This is a way of honoring my impact on the future.

Aside from pictures of family or favored items of self-expression, substantial furniture, treasured possessions, family heirlooms, or mementos are fitting articles for the descendants portion of a room.

COMPASSION

When entering an unfamiliar setting, I often find myself searching for something to hang on to. Imagine entering a boss's office and having a table to the right there to lend support and balance as you step inside, a message of concern for those who enter. If we express this care for those around us, they will be more likely to care about us. The ancient Chinese called this area the *helpful people corner*, believing that if the appropriate items were located there people would be likely to help the occupant. The pyramid school shifts the emphasis from "What's in it for me?" to one of compassion for others. Nonetheless, the results will be the same: if you care, you will be cared for.

Look to the compassion corner when entering a home to determine how your needs will be met. In a similar way, be sure to provide assistance to those who enter your world. Both the provider and the recipient will benefit.

A solid piece of waist-high furniture is a most effective item to place in this area. Do not flood this area with light; our transition into a space is made more comfortable when we aren't the immediate center of attention.

Self

Your view of life is determined by your perspective. Children think all grown-ups are giants. Most adults see professional basketball players as huge. If, however, you were standing on top of the Empire State Building, no human being would seem big. It's all a matter of perspective. The point at which you enter a room determines what you see.

If you live in a typical community, you probably drive home from work, shopping, or school. Many times you drive your car directly into a garage before entering your home. The garage door becomes a front entrance and probably leads into a utility room or kitchen. What

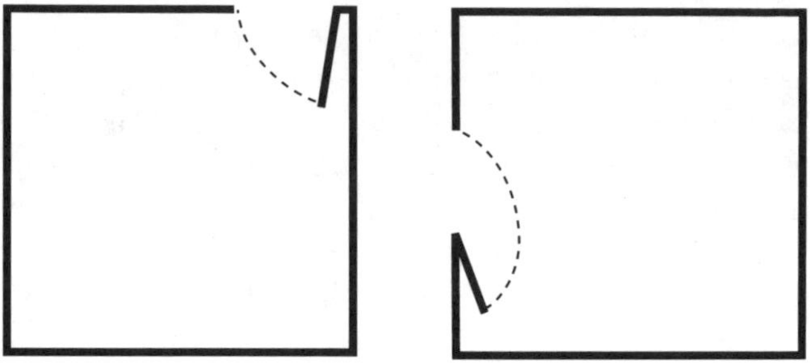

Doors should open flat against an adjoining wall.

an entrance! In many cases a garage door entrance is awkward and unattractive and does not propel the occupant to the heart of the home. Certainly it's not what the architect intended as the home's first impression.

Whether it's the architectural front door or another entrance, however, where a home or individual room is entered most frequently is the front door. That is where we assign the aspect of self in a ba-gua overlaid on an entire home or a room. The self is the door to all experiences, and you and it are one at a threshold of a room.

Make sure that an entrance passageway is not crowded, forcing you to squeeze inside. Ideally the door should open flat against an adjoining wall, and nothing should be stored behind it. In addition, this vantage point should grant an unobstructed view of the entire room.

Controls for lighting and temperature are best positioned by an entrance. I have a friend who lives in a home that has gone through numerous renovations. The entrance has changed a few times, and an electrical switch to light the room was not always provided at the threshold. Therefore, many times, when returning home at night, my friend and her company have stumbled across the room in search of a light switch.

The element of earth grounds us. Place objects made with earth near the entrance. Ceramic planters, a tile floor, or landscape paintings can have the benefit of grounding us when entering and connecting us to the outside natural world.

Wisdom

Where the traditional school of feng shui assigned a section of a room to knowledge, the pyramid school favors the concept of wisdom, which is more complex. Knowing things and extrapolating the impact of their meaning is what separates knowledge from wisdom. It is wisdom, the alignment of experience with insight, that propels us successfully through life.

Learning materials such as books, magazines, and newspapers are appropriate in this area, as is a comfortable solitary chair for thinking and contemplating. Since metal objects represent mental process, place metal objects in this area to sharpen one's wisdom. Fountains or products constructed with glass can represent one's resolve to stay the course until knowledge evolves into wisdom.

Community

Community is a second level of family and consists of topography, the configuration of buildings and roads, and the people who create a thread of connection through common practices. Schools, traffic rules, ordinances, and informal networks of clubs, sports teams, and service organizations are supports included in the structure called *community*.

To live a life with Taoist intent, honoring community as a second tier of family is a must. A metal object placed in this position best speaks to the intention of community, for metal is formed by absorbing the content of the earth. Its existence depends on what was in the soil, but its life is independent of its original source, the same way that community contains the ingredients of our life's experience but we individuals function independently.

POWER

In many ways ancient feng shui focused its attention on business and wealth because wealth was considered the measure of a successful life. Today, however, we acknowledge that happiness can come from other life satisfactions like family, ideas, or personal endeavors. True satisfaction lies in feeling actualized, and we are empowered when we are all we can be. So personal power, not wealth, is a better cornerstone to build from in our quest for contentment.

The power corner of a room is the one farthest from the entrance door to the left to echo our biological past, our flight-or-fight response. Humans living in caves or one-room dwellings had time to react to predators when positioned farthest from an entrance. In the same way,

Power and relationship corners

a desk positioned correctly in a power corner affords both a view of the door and maximum time to react to anyone entering the room.

If a room is entered from the center, the power corner is on the left. If a room is entered on the left, the far left side becomes compromised so the right-hand side of the room assumes the position for both the power and the relationship areas. Similarly, if the entrance to the room is on the far right, then the far left-hand corner acts as the position for both power and relationship.

To improve a power corner in a home, place a photograph of you competing in a 10K run or a seashell recovered from a beach while on a memorable vacation. In an office, a diploma, a successful advertising campaign, or a sales chart can be both inspirational and motivating.

In both cases a power corner must be clean and organized. I have often walked into offices to discover a power corner piled high with papers. In those cases I advise the occupants either to organize the papers or to remove them from sight. If they follow only this one piece of advice, I assure them, they will be amazed at how much this one will positively alter their ability to be effective.

A bright light, a wooden table, a low cabinet or object, or a shiny surface that catches the eye would be an appropriate object for the power corner. Do not put a mirror in that location. We tend to be self-critical and focus attention on ourselves when passing by a mirror's reflection. We need to be focused on the activity at hand, not our physical self, in this area.

What surrounds us ultimately enters us. If a TV is a room's spiritual or physical center, then you are promoting passivity rather than activity. Make sure the focal point of a room matches its intention. Just as a healthy lifestyle promotes a happier life, securing the highest and best purpose for each room in a home is a way to ensure an optimum life. Pick and choose symbols, and place them where they will induce you to the best you can be.

7

The Senses: Sight, Sound, Smell, and Touch

The pyramid school views cultural interpretations and physiological reactions to conditions in the physical world as important.

Sight

"Seeing is believing" is an adage that underscores how important we consider our visual world. So much of our information is processed through our eyes, yet sight is not an absolute. We see what we know and learn to see what is familiar.

A child's initial visual connection to the world, for example, is his or her caregiver, and very few other visual details will manifest themselves in a way that the child understands. In the same way that a child will not recognize different people until they become known, you may not identify the shape of a tree's leaves if unfamiliar with the tree. Although you "see" trees, you do so in a generic way and cannot easily distinguish one tree from another. Seeing is determined by familiarity as much as physiological processes. You can't assume something is seen just because it is there. Therefore, if you want to be sure some object is noticed, surround it with movement, additional light, or bright colors. For example, if you want to take time out to read more books, place bright light on a bookshelf and place a red object on the shelf beside the books.

Light is the source that defines shape, depth, and color, and highlighting important areas in a home is the simplest, most effective way to effect change. What we notice is where we'll go.

Colors

By understanding the emotional context of colors we can manipulate the experience of place to our benefit. Colors engage our eyes as well as our cultural interpretations of emotional experiences. Black, a color that absorbs all others, represents death in the West. We believe that at the moment of death we are rewarded or penalized by the accumulation of our life's virtues or transgressions. On the other hand, Chinese wear white to symbolize death, which summarizes their philosophy on physical extinction. White does not absorb any color; it reflects all. In death, the Chinese believe, we are released from life's accumulated energies and begin the process of growth and change for another lifetime.

By adding or reducing a color, its intensity, or its purity, you can adjust a setting to complement its intent. For example, no one would decorate a hospital room all black in a Western culture, nor would an all-white room be appropriate for a young child. But reducing black to an accent color and softening it to a gray could be appropriate in a healing setting, as would adding colored pigment to white, intensifying it into pale yellow, rose, or sky blue for a child's room.

This section will define the experience of color, the range of emotional extremes, and how to use color in a setting. Color can express personality and should be used in the same way you select your wardrobe.

I have a friend who likes the color orange; not the kind of orange you find on a Popsicle; this wouldn't suit her, for she is complex and exotic. A muted darkened mango orange matches her personality. When selecting a color, find the shade, tone, and temperament of a color that reflects you as well as the experience you intend for the space.

Remember also that colors can have both positive and negative meanings. While a single red rose on a dining room table symbolizes elegance and beauty, the notion of a red-light district implies an offensiveness.

Red

Red, being the color of blood, represents a flow of life's forces. When we add this color to a setting, we are affirming life on a deep level. Red can be a springboard from which activity, responses, and focus commence. It produces the long wave at the extreme end of the visible spectrum and a strong human reaction.

Red can register as overpowering. Our eyes are drawn to this color, and it is often the first one noted in a perceptible field. Moreover, it is associated with violence and can agitate as well as deplete a feeling of comfort. In all cases pure red will elicit a powerful reaction, and an awareness of its potency is paramount to its effective use.

Note: Continuums of interpretation indicate the extremes conveyed by each color. Either limit the exposure to the extremes, use the midrange of a color, or provide the opposite for balance.

Use Red To . . .

Denote extremes, as in a red stop light
Distract, as in a toreador's cape in a bullfight
Warn, as in a lifeguard's red flag
Mark a ceremonial activity, as in red ribbons at opening ceremonies
Agitate, as do carnivals' flashing red lights
Warm, as does sitting next to the glowing embers of a fire
Attract attention, as in a bull's eye in a target
Signal approaching an important area, as does a red carpet

Stay Away From Pure Red . . .

In mental institutions
In contemplative areas such as bedrooms or offices
In sports facility lobbies
In crowded public facilities (rest rooms or elevators)

Yellow

Yellow is the color of the sun, which is an important element of life on earth just as the center of an egg is the epicenter of life for many species. In some cultures gold represents wealth. Wealth in biological or material terms starts with a notion of plenty—enough sunlight or enough money.

The macula lutea of the eye is a small yellowish area slightly off center from the retina that makes up the region of maximum visual acuity. Yellow can clarify perception.

In our culture yellow is often associated with negative attributes such as rumor mongering (yellow journalism) and cowardice (yellow bellied). Paper yellows when it ages. A yellowish tint in the whites of the eyes suggests an unhealthy condition. In addition, we perceive a person's face as unattractive when cast in a yellow light.

Life fulfilling ⟵⟶ Life collapsing

Use Yellow To . . .

Cheer, as does sunshine
Infuse with hope, as do golden opportunities
Vitalize a work area with light
Elevate mental activity, as does meditating on a point of light
Counter the effects of diminished daylight
Warm, in the same way as reflection from polished gold
Activate explorations, as did the yellow brick road in *The Wizard of Oz*

Stay Away from Pure Yellow . . .

In nightclubs
That reflects on faces
Inside cupboards or drawers
In bathrooms
In a room for meditation

Blue

Sky and water cover the globe with the color blue. These unknowns puzzle us and invite exploration. Blue is a color of isolation and adventure. Interestingly, it is also the most popular color choice of American males. Are they not taught to be independent and investigative?

Yet if the skin becomes bruised, it turns blue. A blue movie or blue joke connotes profanity. When we are extremely exasperated, we are described as "blue in the face." Blue, like all colors, has one foot kicking open a positive door and the other a negative one.

Striving toward mystery, adventure	←→	Advancing toward negativity

Use Blue To . . .

Denote mystery, as do the deep blue seas
Assist with meditation, as does the sky to contemplation
Express uniqueness, as does "once in a blue moon"
Cool, as blue waters can on a hot day
Attend to seriousness of purpose, as when I wore a navy blue suit to my college interviews

Stay Away from Pure Blue . . .

When a space needs to be cheerful
When a space needs agitation
In cold places
In dining areas
On paths for general use

Orange

Orange is the fusion of the visible red blood of human life (blood is blue until it mixes with oxygen) and the sun's yellow. Midway between yellow and red, it absorbs the characteristics of both. However, orange is not a popular overall color for interiors because of the confusing symbolism between a human being's life-sustaining entity (blood) and the world's life-sustaining entity (the sun). Many cultures elevate human activity above the natural universe and consequently use red more than both yellow and orange.

Fusion	←→	Burial

Use Orange To . . .

Fuse person to place, as red and yellow fuse earth to human life
Sustain conversation or thought, as enlightenment needs awareness
Define spirituality, as do a monk's saffron robes
Refine a sense of commitment
Repel loneliness

Stay Away from Pure Orange . . .

When autocratic leadership is needed
When complete rest is needed
When concentrated focus is required

Green

Lying between blue and yellow, the color green evokes a consciousness of life. Where there is green, there is life-sustaining human habitation. It is not coincidental that green vegetables provide exquisite nutrition for the human body. Green, the color of most vegetation, when brought into an interior space connects us to nature. We feel alive and rejuvenated because we associate green with growth.

Green can also indicate immaturity, as in the immature apple. Having insufficient training or being too new is expressed by the term *greenhorn*. Envy, that deadly sin, is described as green. When we turn green, we are nauseated; hence green can be a sign of sickness.

Connection ⟷ Disconnection

Use Green To . . .

Connect us to nature
Create peaceful conditions, as does a houseplant

Nurture, as in the description of a gardener as having a green thumb
Rejuvenate, as in making something green
Promote rest or calm
Indicate something new in the same way we call young onions green

Stay Away from Green . . .

Where growth is undesirable (facilities treating cancer patients)
Inside moving vehicles

White

White is the reflection of all colors. It cannot be influenced by anything. It connotes innocence because it is untainted; nothing but self is present.

Since white diffuses all color and remains pure, godliness is often associated with the color white. White surrounds the egg and the seeing part of the eye, and it is an appropriate wrapper for life itself.

White can be experienced as counterrevolutionary or taking a stance against the status quo because it makes all other things stand out. Nothing can be hidden when surrounded by white. White is a good color to wear to a job interview because it shows you have nothing to hide.

Purity ←→ Emptiness

Use White To . . .

Define a focused ego, as does a white shirt for business attire
Identify purity, as in a bridal gown

Convey cleanliness and freshness
Show there is nothing to hide

Stay Away from Pure White . . .

In cold climates
In theaters or movie interiors
In places where people don't know each other
In student lounges
In funeral homes, waiting rooms and children's bedrooms

Black

Ah, the magic and mystery of black! We feel absorbed and are absorbing when we wear black. I once had a female client from Texas who, after a normal feng shui consultation, asked me why so many people asked her why she always wore black. Could I explain why they seemed uncomfortable with her choice?

The traditional South's social conditions bade females to be simple and helpful, not enigmatic. Black is the color of mystery. It says, "If you want to know me, find out for yourself!" In some situations the mystery and magic of black is sexy, and in some places it causes discomfort.

Totally absorbing, black reveals nothing and does little to brighten. Black requires our eyes to strain and communicates, "You figure it out."

Mysterious ⟷ Strange

Use Black To . . .

Assert independence
Evoke intrigue and mystery, as did the lady in black

Radiate warmth because it feels absorbing
Express strength and solidarity

Stay Away from Pure Black . . .

In children's spaces
In healing spaces
When forthright communication is needed
In service areas
In reading areas

Purple

Purple is not a simple combination of blue and red. It is a hard color to mix, created only when blue is mixed with certain shades of magenta. This difficulty is reflected by its regal use. It's hard and rare to be a leader just as it's hard to mix purple. To come forth with insights requires us to dig deep inside and believe in our egotistical view of the world. Purple evokes self centeredness and spirituality

Rage is the flip side of asserting oneself calmly with grace. The expression "purple with rage" connotes purple's negative message.

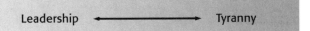

Leadership ←——→ Tyranny

Use Purple To . . .

Evoke higher mental processes
Signify power
Elevate self-esteem

Stay Away from Purple . . .

In egalitarian settings
In boiler or war rooms or where egos can clash

Scientists are learning more and more about the physical effects of color. After World War II, the navy spent time trying to discern what color was best suited for the stressful conditions inside submarines. The research showed that bubblegum pink induces calmness and serenity, and today the same color is being used experimentally to help calm highly charged teens in juvenile detention centers. No matter how excited and overly stressed, after ten minutes in a bubblegum pink room enraged detainees usually stop yelling and screaming. After twenty or more minutes a statistically significant number of teens are dozing or sleeping. Bubblegum pink has sedative effects.

The pyramid school tells us to go with our feelings, not a prescribed notion of fashion, to determine which color should be augmented or reduced. When we touch a chord within, we usually are responding on all levels—culturally, biologically, and socially.

Sound

Few parents consider the sounds heard blasting from their teenagers' music source to be harmonic. In this bone of contention between the generations what is sheer noise to the parents is melodic to the children. The distinction between these experiences is personal preference and control.

There is a charming ice cream shop in my neighborhood that draws in crowds from miles around. Even though the space is dotted with tables dressed in fanciful red checked cloths, most customers leave the store to eat on a bumpy, cold stone wall outside. The culprit is the overpowering churning gurgle of the motor that keeps the ice cream cold. No one can stand it! When I asked the owners if they could tolerate this din, they replied that they didn't even notice it. This made sense when I realized that I hardly notice the sound of my lawn mower when I'm behind it, but the distant hum of a neighbor's mower can wake me out of my Sunday reverie. The difference is the control over an experience. When we control a sound, we rarely experience it as negative.

Biologically, sound connects us with others in our environment. When we're out of sight our vocal idiom expresses us. Out of sight is out of mind only when there is silence. A parent's voice can soothe a fussy child even before the parent picks the child up. In the womb a fetus hears sounds through the amniotic fluid that are later associated with safety and nurturing. Experiments show that when baby monkeys are given an artificial mother with a clock inside, the sound, similar to a heartbeat, keeps these baby monkeys calmer and less agitated than ones with a clockless surrogate mother. It has also been postulated that young animals cry so their parents can locate them as well as know they are safe. The difference between a pleasant chirp and a panicked one gives a mother bird some indication of whether her babies are safe from predators.

Nature is never silent. Wind moves vegetation so that leaves rustle, branches moan, and grasses swish. Those sounds, along with the utterances of all animals, make up a mix of sound that is hardly noticed, linking us subtly to other life.

Too little sound ⟷ Too much sound

Note: Continuum of interpretation indicates the extremes conveyed by sound. Either limit the exposure to the extremes or provide the opposite for balance. The right mix of extremes with a lion's share of experience center between the two.

On the other hand, too much noise puts our nervous system on alert, a fact TV advertisers are well aware of when they raise the volume of commercials above that of the other programming. High volume is appropriate as an attention-getting device. The words "order in the court" might go unnoticed, for example, without the crashing of a gavel on a hard wooden surface. Unfortunately, when loud sounds are sustained we begin to call them *noise*, which ultimately wears us down.

We have many ways of controlling sound for our own purposes. No ceremony is complete without sound. Be it a band heralding the arrival of a parade or the ringing of bells to signal meditation, sound is often integrated into events. What would a graduation ceremony be without the strains of "Pomp and Circumstance" or a wedding without "Here Comes the Bride"?

Sound can also be used to agitate and invigorate. What parade is complete without a marching band? The beat of the music keeps the energy going and spirits high. Concert organizers know that a warm-up band is needed to ready a crowd for the main event.

Controlling Sound to Benefit Us

Reducing stimulation can foster behavior change, as parents know and act on when they tell an out-of-control child, "Go to your room." Many religions use retreats to foster contemplation. In our homes a quiet bedroom might be the antidote to the hustle and bustle of a household's activities.

On the other hand, the feeling of isolation experienced by many older people living alone can be mitigated by introducing sound. Often when I am asked to create spaces for the elderly, I recommend a bubbling fish tank or fountain or suggest placing a small fan at the base of a plant to make its leaves rustle.

Children also need sound to reassure them. As an infant, my son Zachary would listen for what seemed like hours to a musical mobile above his crib. When the music ran out before he drifted into slumber, he would vociferously relate his objection.

A silent home can feel unhappy, while a noisy home can cause tension. Finding a balance between the two is the challenge before us. Whether a space leans toward silence or sound depends on the activities for which we use it. The following list can serve as a guide in determining which to include in a space.

Use Sound to Initiate . . .

Relaxation
Ceremony
Concentration
Emotion

Use Sound to Reverse . . .

Sadness
Nervousness
Anger

Appropriate Indoor Sounds

Fans
Bubbling water
Wind-sensitive objects such as leaves, chimes, or curtains
Music

SMELL

The sense of smell is connected to the oldest part of the brain. It is the only sense that we cannot re-create. We are able to close our eyes and see a loved one's face, concentrate and hear the strains of a Mozart concerto, or slide our cheek over an imaginary piece of velvet; but try to sniff the air and experience the smell of bacon frying or a lilac in bloom. It can't be done in quite the same way.

But a particular smell can trigger a past experience. My first dolls were stuffed with cotton fibers, and today, when I'm removing laundry from a dryer, the smell of cotton triggers memories of my childhood. I "see" my room, "feel" as if I am sitting on my carpet, and "taste" the doll's hair as I held it between my teeth to wet the ends for curling. Smells bring back an entire scene. I ponder whether my son, whose toys were most often plastic, will reminisce about his childhood someday when inhaling a whiff of another synthetic product.

"The nose knows" is not merely a cute aphorism but a sage maxim. Early on, a fetus's olfactory stimulation controls the rate of swallowing. Infants identify their caretakers by smell as much as sight. Aromatherapy's value is becoming more and more accepted today as science uncovers how smells impact on health. The smell of spiced apples has been found effective in lowering blood pressure. Are lavender and old lace really a capricious twosome? Lavender has been discovered to be antiaphrodisiac. Maybe that's why elderly women have a propensity for its scent!

Use fragrances in a beneficial way to reduce or enhance behavior.

Benefits from Common Scents

Spiced apples lower blood pressure.

Basil cheers and is good for reducing the influence of migraines.

Cedar dispels fear.

Eucalyptus clears the sinuses and reduces emotional overload.

Frankincense is conducive to prayer or mediation.

Geranium relieves premenstrual tension and is an antidepressant.

Jasmine mitigates emotional suffering.

Lime and lemon elevate mood and fight exhaustion and listlessness.

Mint helps eliminate mental fatigue and unclear thinking.

Orange helps us feel warmer and less self-conscious.

Pine strengthens and cleanses.

Rose strengthens inner being.

Sandalwood helps raise our spirits.

Thyme purifies.

Verbena is cooling and mildly sedating.

Ylang-ylang has an aphrodisiac effect. It can also sedate and relieve hypertension.

Try these scents for the following areas:

Children's bedrooms: basil, cedar, orange, pine

	Antidepressants	Sedatives	Stimulants	Deodorants	Hypnotics	Clarifiers
sage	X	X		X		X
geranium	X		X			
jasmine	X					
lavender	X	X	X	X	X	
sandalwood	X	X				
eucalyptus			X	X		
lime			X			X
cedar		X				
spiced apples		X				X
pine			X			X
mint			X			X
cinnamon					X	

Couple's bedroom: ylang-ylang, jasmine
Gathering rooms: thyme, sandalwood, orange
Studies: eucalyptus, lime, lemon, mint
Offices: thyme, verbena, jasmine
Hotel lobbies: thyme, lavender, geranium
Airplanes: verbena, lavender, sage
Physicians' waiting rooms: sage, lavender, cedar

Touch

Experience is enhanced by touch. Holding a stuffed animal can catapult us back to childhood when we snuggled up to a soft fluffy critter as we drifted off to sleep.

Nerve endings in the skin alert us to react. Letting go of a scorching pot handle is an automatic response. But trembling in anticipation of the touch of a beloved's lips is purely cultural. In both cases the experience of touch communicates information and elicits feelings. How we use proximity, fabric, and the surfaces of flooring, walls, and cabinetry in our living spaces may affect our experience of place only subtly but is nonetheless consequential.

Whether it's gliding a finger over a feathery expanse of velvet pile or rubbing a cheek on a smooth silk pillow, certain materials can conjure up emotional responses. Bring a festive mood to an otherwise ordinary day by using a cut crystal goblet as a water glass. Touch can be a handmaiden of emotional experience.

Sometimes even an appearance of texture can elevate a mood. To lift your spirits and thwart depression, place a rose by your table setting. To consecrate erudition, buy a set of leatherbound books for your shelves. Place a vase filled with peacock feathers in a foyer to signal welcome. Even the sight of a known pleasant texture can awaken an intended response.

POSITIVE	NEGATIVE
soothe emotions	repel activity
relax	hurt
energize	lull
direct us to an emotional place	conjure up past negative experiences

Touch Can . . .

Grasping a polished bronze doorknob can ready us to enter a place of importance, while opening a door with a thin lightweight aluminum latch can produce the opposite feeling. Gauge how it feels or how it appears to feel when considering choices in a home. Delighting your sense of touch can elevate your mood.

Part II

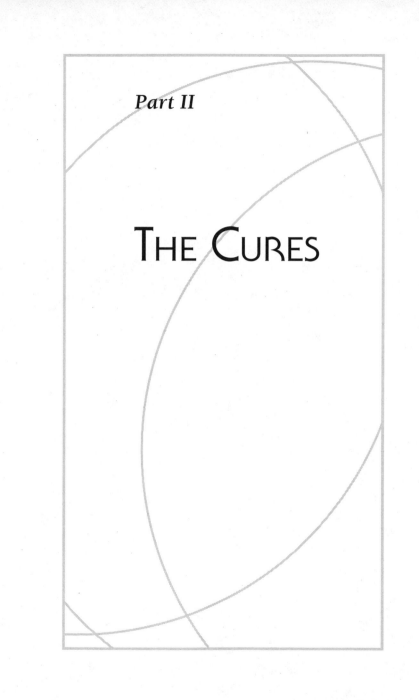

The Cures

This part of the book is divided into four sections: outdoors, architectural details, individual rooms, and special considerations. Take the test in each chapter to identify the areas that need adjusting so you can elevate your home's feng shui quotient. Each unfavorable condition will be followed by an explanation of why it is troublesome, then suggestions for bringing about a cure. Step by step, you will uncover effective and easy ways to correct ill situations.

Don't despair if you uncover many areas to remedy. Just as there are no hopeless situations, there are no perfect ones. The worst can become better, and the acceptable can be improved. But don't read the information in Part II the way a first-year medical student reads *Merck Medical Manual*. You can't possibly have every illness!

The process of evolving is ongoing. As life shifts, so should the spaces in which you live be adjusted to harmonize with current needs. Today's cure may not be as effective tomorrow, and what once was a perfect space can become inadequate over time.

The cures suggested here are merely springboards. Know that you can be inventive and experimental. If one way does not seem to work, kick it aside and try another. How long you should wait for a cure to be effective is about as long as you would wait for a seed to sprout up from the earth. A cure grows like a plant, and if success doesn't rear its head and thrive, sow another seed.

My mother and I are as different as two languages when it comes to recuperating from an illness. I'm the kind that jumps out of bed hours after surgery and traipses around the hospital, dragging my IV behind me. My mom is the kind to eavesdrop on medical students making their rounds, listening to them discuss her potentially fatal condition. Armed with this information, she lies in wait to confer with her doctor about remedies for her condition. Her way of getting better is to focus intensely on her illness; my way is to treat it as if it had never happened. The bottom line is that we both eventually get well. The moral of this story is: whatever works for you is best.

Remember, intention is the beginning of change. You have already started on the road to transformation by selecting this book. The thrill of starting a journey is knowing that you are already on the road to a desired destination.

A Word About the Tests

The tests are guides to help you pinpoint the areas in your home that need improvement. All points are negative. If you score points, go to the section in the chapter that describes how to correct the problem you've identified.

Again, don't be discouraged by a high negative score. Life is often best for those who had to work hard to get what they want. When things come easily, we often don't prevail on ourselves to seize opportunity. Those who dare to evaluate and confront change with energy and intention can, in the end, succeed beyond their wildest dreams.

A Word About the Cures

There are ten categories of remedies. The exact object used is not as important as the category it fulfills. For example, light-reflecting objects can be as commonplace as a mirror or as exotic as chrome trim. Use the list of remedies as a guideline to select the item that will mesh best with your aesthetics.

Categories of Remedies

1. Repositioning of Furniture

Rearranging furniture in a room is the quickest and often the most effective way of implementing change. First impressions are hard to forget, and what is first seen in a room often sets the tone and feeling for the experience. If a desk is the first object you see when entering an office, you probably waste no time sitting down to work. If the desk is in a corner or out of first sight, you may find yourself dawdling before beginning to labor.

By simply moving objects around in your home, you will make immense changes in how your living spaces are experienced. For example, to augment your resolve to diet, place an object, like a table, in the middle of a direct path to your refrigerator. To retrieve snacks, you will then have to circumvent both the table and your resolve. Those extra moments may give your willpower time to override an action that could interfere with reaching your goal.

2. Light

The objects included within a pool of light are similar to those illuminated by a spotlight on a stage: light forces attention on them.

Even personal power can be affected by lighting. For example, parents who are losing control over teenage children can increase their effectiveness through subtle lighting shifts over the parents' seats in an overhead fixture. If the fixture has four bulbs, use sixty watts over the teenagers' seat and a hundred watts over the parents'. With only wall illumination, shift seating so that the parents will be near the wall light.

3. Color

Color used alone or in patterns can alter the mood of persons entering a space. A feeling of exuberance can be quieted by a room decorated with subdued colors, while a depressed person can rebound in a bubblegum pink or sunflower yellow room. The amounts of color—their hues, tones, and shades—can influence one's emotional response to a place.

4. Plants

The color, shape, and texture of plants can reinforce aspects of the other cures as well as the five elements. For example, a small-leafed plant placed by an open window or near a heating or cooling vent can serve as a movement cure by virtue of its ability to quiver in gusts of air, while a pointed leaf can be used as a symbol of the fire element. In all cases, plants unite us with the world outside and instill feeling of being part of the whole.

5. Movement

Any object that initiates action is classified as movement. Potential to move can be as potent as actual motion. Therefore, a passageway filled with people, an open window, heating and cooling vents, and wind-sensitive objects are appropriately considered movement, as are cuckoo clocks, fans, chimes, and mechanical devices.

6. Reflective Surfaces

Any item that can duplicate an image in another location—mirrors, polished metals, glass, TV and computer screens, and nonagitated water—fits this category.

7. Heavy Objects

Sculpture, pedestals, tables, chairs, sofas, area rugs, desks, benches, boulders, recirculating fountains, and cabinets are among the objects that fit into this category.

8. Sound

Sound can be created artificially, as in the case of music played with instruments, TV, cars, engines, telephones, bells, and tools or as by-products of natural phenomena, like the utterances of living creatures or the earth erupting and shifting. Sound is produced by the movement of vegetation, water, rain, wind, or critters scurrying around doing the business of living.

9. Water

Water is central to our existence. Our first home, the uterus, floats us in a waterlike atmosphere. Without water our corporeal being would perish. Its presence in a pristine condition is crucial to our physical and emotional health.

10. Maintenance

Cleaning up areas in your home can be a first step toward cleaning up parts of your life. If you do nothing else, look around and tidy the messiest or least organized area of your home. By throwing out what is not used and organizing what is you will make a quantum leap toward future successes. In all cases cleaning, tidying, and organizing will benefit your life. After completing that task, I guarantee, you will notice positive changes in your life.

The Cures

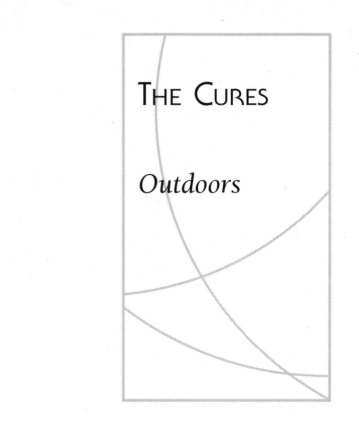

Outdoors

8

Geology, Topography, and Direction

We can't respond appropriately to someone without knowing them. In the same way, to understand the places in which we live we need to know some details about the shape, location, and composition of our place on this sphere.

Changing the form of our earth can affect the natural intention of place. When we fill in swamps, raze hills, or block sunlight with tall buildings, we are creating unnatural conditions that either will be undermined by nature, the way storms tear down sea walls, or will wear down those who have to maintain them.

Being cognizant of where the sun rises and sets and the time frames for each room's use might uncover reasons for liking or disliking certain rooms. A sun-filled breakfast nook positioned with windows on the east side of a home will feel very different from one with windows facing north.

Doctors of the vital force, the Chinese description for feng shui practitioners, often tasted the soil at a building's site. Knowledge of the soil's alkaline or acid content, mineral deposits, and texture contributed to choices of building materials and construction style. For example, post and beam construction might need certain modifications to prevent shifting or sinking in grainy or loosely packed soil.

Before you start evaluating the inside of your living space, see if there are influences in the world surrounding you that you have not considered before.

TEST

SCORE 1 if your home's entrance faces north.

SCORE 2 if a room used for study in the afternoon faces west.

SCORE 1 if sunshine is blocked from the breakfast area or a main gathering room.

SCORE 2 if your home is on the incline of a steep street.

SCORE 2 if there are harmful deposits underneath your land.

SCORE 2 if the soil surrounding your home will not easily support plant life.

SCORE 1 if any rock ledge is exposed in your foundation.

The total negative score could be 11. Naturally, curing all negative conditions is the ideal to strive toward. If you have scored almost one half of the total score, consider it a warning signal and attend to making some changes as soon as possible. Being surrounded by the best conditions helps you thrive!

If you have a front door facing north . . .

Sunlight is a stimulant. Sunlight produces a chemical reaction that induces optimism, hope, and cheer. A sun-filled exit helps get your day off to a good start.

If you have a choice, leave your home each morning through a door facing east or south, even if it is not the main door of the home. If you don't, infuse the area with cheer by planting flowers with red blooms, painting a birdhouse yellow, or placing in your visual path some object that makes you smile.

I lived in the part of northern New Jersey that has the same weather patterns as Buffalo, New York (it's called the *snow belt* for a good reason!). In winter my son would plant a mannequin's arm outside our front door. It was his fun way of keeping track of the snow's depth. Even when the weather was frigid and dreary for days on end, each time I left my house I would smile at the sight of the mannequin's arm. Find a unique way to put some sunshine in your day as you leave home.

If you have a study facing the afternoon sun . . .

The sinking afternoon sun puts a strain on our psyche when most of us have already been up for about half our waking day. Sitting by a window during that time is an encumbrance to optimum performance if you're engaged in exacting work.

If there is no alternative to moving your activity from a western window, place a filtering screen between you and the glare. A plant, a screen, a framed stain-glass piece, or any perforated item can be an effective shield between the sun's glare and your eyes.

If you have a breakfast area or main room without sunlight . . .

Sunlight is earth's energizing force and facilitates internal or external activity. It controls disposition and dissipates disease. We need light to encourage optimal performance in many areas and to maintain overall health. Sunlight is desirable in rooms where we spend most of our time, particularly early mornings.

Staying outdoors for most of the daylight hours was how native Alaskans thwarted depression during the short days of winter. Only when they assimilated the ways of the lower states and started remaining indoors to work was there an increase in despair and depression.

When going outside is impossible, increase the intensity of electric lights, adorn surfaces with fruits or vegetables, and infuse the decor with brightly colored objects. Add movement by placing wind-sensitive objects by doors and air vents and increase background sounds with music or sounds from clocks, fans, or chimes. Infusing a space with energy is a way to simulate the outdoors.

If your home is positioned midway on a steep incline . . .

In the same way a ball will not stop rolling until it reaches the bottom of a hill, chi or energy will pass by a home situated midway down an incline. Moreover, leaving a home situated in the middle of a steep slope requires you to brake or strain to begin your journey.

Increase the visual presence of a home midway up a hill. Eyes should be riveted on the home, not the hill, by form, color, or light. Additional lights on the entrance's pathway will benefit a nighttime approach. Bold-colored vegetation, a patterned walkway that widens as it reaches the street, or a door painted a color that contrasts with the rest of a home will pull in the chi.

Just as time on a treadmill will fly by if we are engrossed in conversation, it is easier to surmount difficulties when otherwise pleasantly engaged. Sighting pleasant details can mitigate a trudge up the steps to reach an entrance door.

If your house is built near harmful mineral deposits . . .

On a mountaintop in northern New Jersey a series of homes was built over uranium deposits. In addition to the physical illnesses that living over harmful mineral deposits caused, the consequent emotional stress had a domino effect, giving these folks more than their share of suffering.

Polluted waters, harmful mineral deposits, and caustic fumes spewing from a factory's chimney can also prevent vegetation from thriving.

Responsible builders will shoulder the burden of analyzing land for safety. But don't rely on others exclusively. Investigate, via the local library, the area's geological conditions and potential hazards before moving in.

Whether you employ a company or do it yourself, there are ways to find out whether you are living with emissions of harmful substances like radon, polluted waters, or polluted air. Vacuum out harmful gases from underneath the foundation, purify your drinking water, and filter noxious air to secure the healthiest atmosphere for you and your family.

But don't stop there. Fighting these conditions on an individual basis is expensive and wearing. Be part of the solution. Go to the source and work to make changes. Fight for ordinances that require tests for radon prior to building on a site and force industry to refrain from dumping pollutants into the air and water. Boycott companies that won't stop. Write letters to the editor of your local paper to inform citizens of problems. United we can change conditions; divided we lose.

If you have land that will not support vegetation . . .

Have you ever noticed a variation in density of vegetation on a mountainside? Parts of a hillside where vegetation thrives and places where vegetation barely clings to life? You can read this scene like a doctor diagnoses a patient. There is a reason some areas do not support thick vegetation. Those areas should be investigated when selecting a building site.

The reason for the land's inability to support vegetation may be harmful. Investigate before you carve out your castle.

If you have a basement with an exposed rock ledge . . .

Exposed rock ledges as a part of a foundation can precipitate drainage problems. No rock formation is airtight or watertight, and often in spring the fissures in the rock become a conduit for water.

If an even foundation cannot be secured, it is better to construct a home with posts and beams in lieu of a cement slab.

If you live in a home that has an exposed rock ledge as part of the foundation, seal all surfaces of the rock with watertight paints and plant water-loving vegetation outside on the home's perimeter. While on the one hand, you will be battling the forces that be, on the other you will be rendering newly planted vegetation a service by feeding it via the altered watercourse. Fight a negative with a positive.

9

The Outdoors Environment and View

The outdoors lures us like bees to a flower. When we feel connected to the world, we feel content. Vegetation, rocks, and water are likely to be a natural part of a scene viewed from a suburban or rural window, but urban settings require special attention. This chapter will help town and city dwellers interpret feng shui's outdoor considerations.

We are influenced by what we see, whether mountains, suburban lawn, or cityscape. The need to be connected to vibrant, pulsating natural aspects of life is just as important to those who live in cities as trees, flowers, and gardens are to the suburbanite or rural dweller. Looking out at a revered landmark building, for example, is a positive outdoor feature for a city dweller in the same way as a hardy ancient oak tree is to those in the country. Living with a view of healthy structures can be a substitute for trees, rocks, or water.

The city offers many possibilities. The shape of buildings can be compared to vegetation. Traffic signals, signs, and people introduce color to a landscape in the same way a grouping of red roses does on a suburban lawn. Glass windows can substitute for water.

Squint your eyes and look at the images from each window. Are they friendly? Do they dominate a view? The shapes and distances of other buildings can be viewed as you might trees in a forest. If they are too close, they might feel oppressive, while the same building in the distance would be just fine.

I used to live on the fourth floor of a New York City apartment complex. From my bedroom window I would gaze out at a line of bathrooms in the adjacent building. Over time I did view the city life as a drain on my life and sought the wide horizons of rural life. Perhaps had my view soared over fanciful rooftops, I would have seen endless possibilities in city life.

TEST

SCORE 1 for any room without a positive view.

SCORE 2 if there is dying vegetation (abandoned or decaying buildings) on your property.

SCORE 1 if vegetation, topography, or neighboring buildings do not form a barrier in the direction of the harshest weather.

SCORE 2 if tall old trees, bushes, or buildings have been razed and no replacements have been planted or the replacements are less valuable, rare, or exotic than what was there before.

SCORE 2 if you can view a polluted water source or dirty windows.

SCORE 1 if you can see a rapidly flowing water source or one that is frequently stagnant or if you can see cracked or painted-over windows.

SCORE 1 if the landscape has no natural adornment.

SCORE 1 if your home is within range of an unkempt lot or tract of land.

The total negative score could be 11. Naturally, curing all negative conditions is the ideal to strive toward. If you have scored almost one half of the total score, consider it a warning signal and attend to making some changes as soon as possible. Being surrounded by the best conditions helps you thrive!

If you have a home without a view of nature . . .

In most cultures isolation is the severest form of punishment. We remove criminals not only from our streets but also from our woodlands, oceans, trees, and lawns. To be sequestered from both nature and our loved ones can be devastating. Why then do we willingly accept living or working in rooms that have no visible connection to the outdoors? Surely we are penalizing ourselves and creating difficult living and working conditions.

I was once called on to cure a massage therapist's windowless room. As the new person in the office, she had been assigned the worst room. She felt claustrophobic and worried about thriving without a window. By installing a grow light over a potted vine, we simulated the outside. We draped greenery across the walls by training potted vines over decorative wall hooks. We hung prints of landscapes and used a wicker desk and chair to give the room a sense of the outdoors. These changes combined a cocoonlike atmosphere with a feeling of connection to the outside. About a year later, when another therapist vacated a room with a window, my client declined the opportunity to move. Her room felt precisely right, and she had no desire to change.

If your property has unhealthy or dying vegetation . . .

The quality of care we give to other life forms often reflects how we care for ourselves. Neglect breeds neglect. We must accept responsibility for allowing conditions that cause harm to exist. Ask yourself what you have done to prevent or stop water pollution, acid rain, car exhaust fumes, and depleted soils, all of which can harm vegetation. Have you voted responsibly or worked in organizations devoted to correcting negative conditions?

Just as there is no substitute for cleanliness but elbow grease, there is only one cure for neglect. When vegetation is ill, you need to discover the cause and remedy it. If direct intervention cannot rectify the problem, try to retard the decline. Consider yourself a guardian for all life forms, for what causes the demise of one will ultimately doom another.

Replace, replace, replace. If a tree dies on your property, plant at least one other. Even better, return more to the earth than has been taken away: plant two or more.

If you live with year-round growing conditions, be sure to replant as the season changes. Here in Florida I replace impatiens, which thrive in our wintertime, with gerbera daisies, which survive summer's heat.

If immediate change seems unlikely because you do not own the site, honor life by caring for a plant inside your own space.

If you have no vegetation or barriers in the direction of the harshest weather . . .

The Chinese believe that a home should face southeast and be backed by a hill or vegetation to the north. This makes perfect sense in China. The severest weather comes from the north, so a home protected this way would be warmer in the winter and drier in spring and summer. Furthermore, the inhabitants would have less wood to chop and more time for family, friends, and relaxation. However, not every location has inclement weather coming from the north. In my home state of Florida we need to protect ourselves from the scorching western sun, which some people accomplish by planting a stand of vegetation to the west. Find the direction of the harshest weather and protect your home from its consequences.

Plant vegetation in the ground or place potted blooms on a balcony, porch, or deck. If outdoor vegetation is not an option, place indoor plants, sculptures, curtains, or any object that will buffer the impact of the severest weather in front of windows facing that direction.

To lessen a cold feeling, position seating away from walls facing the direction of the prevailing winds. Use colors and patterns associated with fire on the curtains, walls, or accessories in these rooms. A flamestitch red and yellow wool afghan is one example of an appropriate accessory on a sofa near a cold wall.

If your neighborhood has lost a healthy ancient tree or building . . .

Achieving a parity between history and the future is the yin and yang that produces optimum conditions here and now. We cannot dispose of or disregard what has evolved in the natural world any more than we can dispose of or disregard our own genetic structure. When we honor, elevate, and sustain that which has been, we duplicate those characteristics in our present lives. Cutting down an ancient tree without replacing it symbolizes a disregard for the threads of our past that connect with the realities of the moment.

If disease, a natural disaster, or the clearing of land for a building causes an ancient tree to be felled, replace it with two or more smaller trees of equal or increased beauty, rarity, or value. If a venerable old building is felled by the boom of a steel ball, find a piece of it and use it as an art object in your home. If you can, photograph the building before it is razed and frame and hang the photo in your home, or donate this piece of the past to the local historical society.

If you have a view of stagnant or polluted water or dirty windows . . .

With water so fundamental to our survival, it should not be surprising that the quality of water near our homes can have repercussions on our lives. A stagnant water source can spawn disease by being a breeding ground for bacteria or insects. Pollution from chemicals used on the soils can contaminate drinking water.

Who can think clearly when confronted by a pile of debris? Viewing polluted water is similar to viewing a mountain of trash. So be sure to shield vital activity in gathering areas from the sight of polluted or stagnant water. Aerating the water in a stagnant pond and adding fish or vegetation capable of absorbing bacteria and pollutants are among the solutions to consider. If the water is not yours to transform, install a fish tank or a small recirculating fountain indoors to shift attention away from the view. In any case, be part of a group whose efforts are directed at eradicating the source of pollution.

If the windows you face are dirty, offer a gift of either elbow grease or money to change the condition.

If you live near or have a view of rapidly flowing water . . .

To some degree, we mimic the messages around us. Living in view of Niagara Falls could exacerbate frenetic activity. The Chinese believe that rapidly flowing water is a simile for dwindling finances. (While water moving too quickly may represent money streaming into your life, it could mean it would flow out just as quickly.)

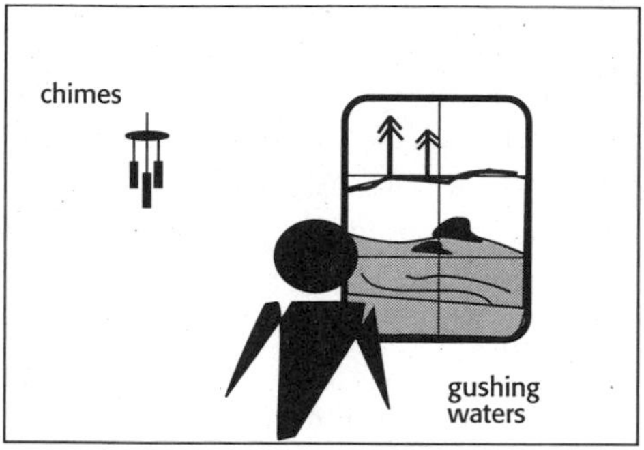

Cure for rapidly flowing waters

If you can see waters moving too quickly outside your window, hang a wall chime near a passageway or a heating duct, or place the fountain or fish tank already mentioned near the window. Any gently moving or sounding object will help.

Contrasting elements render each other more tolerable. Just as we soothe a fussy baby with soft vocal endearments, installing a gently bubbling fountain or fish tank can mitigate the effect of viewing swiftly moving waters outside. The antidote to heat's oppressiveness is cool water. In Palm Springs, for example, tiny pierced conduits emitting light streams of water are draped over palm trees like limp ropes of Christmas lights.

If you are surrounded by a flat, unadorned view . . .

A landscape lacking variety or sufficient vegetation hints at unsuitable living conditions, signals a lack of abundance, and leaves us adrift in a visual void.

I had a friend who didn't leave her house for a year. Succumbing to a devastating emotional trauma, she decided to remain in bed rather than face the world. Calls coaxing her to meet for lunch and pleas from her husband to accompany him on an evening walk fell on deaf ears. In a last-ditch effort to help, I decided to try a feng shui cure. We put a small recirculating fountain in her bedroom as an emotional oasis in her mental desert. We placed colorful blooms in the water and positioned a small fan on the leaves. The water trickled down, the leaves swayed, and her bedroom came alive. Slowly, with this help, my friend's appetite for life returned, and she swung her feet to the floor and her life into action once again.

When changing the landscape outside is not feasible, create a textured miniature indoor landscape. Any location can be transformed by the energy of variation and life.

If you see unkempt lawns or places overgrown with weeds . . .

When I was in college, I had an unhappy roommate who used her closet as a laundry hamper. She would toss in her newly dirtied clothes and quickly slam the door with the back of her heel. It was difficult to keep the mess from spilling out. Eventually her problems became insurmountable, and she sought relief from a therapist, who suggested that her clothes paralleled her emotional state. When she cleaned up the confusion in the closet, she would be ready to deal with her problems. If we do not care for our exterior spaces, how can we care for our interior ones?

If you have not taken the time and energy to maintain your surroundings, do so now. Do it yourself or engage the help of a friend. Every community has an ample supply of high school students who are eager to earn some extra money.

If an unkempt lawn is your neighbor's, offer to lend them a hand. Improving your vista will improve your life as well as your neighbor's.

10

VEGETATION

Vegetation is a container for life and supports us internally and externally. We use it for shelter and comfort and rely on it to supply us with beauty. I grew up next to a forest and spent many days exploring a world filled with tall wooden sentinels. Canopies of leaves, filtering in light, provided a shelter much like a bedsheet tent. My route to school was bordered by colorful plantings displaying the skills of neighborhood gardeners. My mom's best friend had marigolds, a friend's mother, who protected her dyed blond hair under a turban, cultivated her patch with tomatoes, and an exotic French war bride left her territory covered with weeds. I marked my march to school each day by these streetside gardens. A fat oak tree signaled a bend in the road, and my pace quickened to view what was around this curve.

Our connection to vegetation is so ingrained in our psyche that separating it from the panorama of memory becomes difficult. It must be a part of any plan for living. When all around you is swirling with action and energy, it is your yard and/or garden that provides, like the eye of a hurricane, a calm center. A garden is the yin (quiet) for a home's yang (action). A garden or yard can be considered another room, combining the best attributes of a bedroom and a gathering room.

Dennis Fairchild's book *Healing Homes* lists what the ancients believed to be magical properties of different plants. He writes, "The common but potent dandelion, named for the jagged leaves' resemblance to lions' teeth, is governed by the sun. Because its flowers open around 5 A.M. daily and shut at 8 P.M. they served as sundials to shepherds to leave their herds and head home for repose." Families with front lawns graced with this hardy yellow plant are likely to be unencumbered by poor health and protected from calamity.

Similarly, certain attributes have been ascribed to other common plants:

Bamboo—promotes longevity
Evergreen yew—gives protection
Cornflower—encourages balance in love, family, and work relationships
Fern—confers wealth
Geranium—enhances durability for overcoming obstacles
Mint—keeps flying insects from entering a home
Hollyhock—promotes fertility
Yellow rose—encourages lively discussions
Tulip—symbolizes love and devotion

If nothing else, consider a color's effect on your emotions. Review the color section of Chapter 7 or just consider this list:

Red creates positive chi or energy.
Green protects and serves to increase determination.
Yellow clarifies intellectual processes.
Blue reminds us to focus inward.
Black communicates individuality and uniqueness.
White shows you have nothing to hide and are willing to absorb every experience.
Pink summons us to relax.
Purple denotes spirituality.

In your area there may be certain distinctive vegetation that is surrounded by legend. If it feels right, honor it. But also keep in mind that the size of a plant's leaves can satisfy different requirements. Tiny leaves flutter with minimal air movement and can be used in enclosed spaces when the only air currents are created by human movement. Larger leaves can act as a screen or room divider. Vines can soften and drape a severe corner of a wall beam or a furniture's edge. Plants unite us with the world outside and bring green, the color of peace and contentment, indoors.

TEST

SCORE 2 if you do not have any indoor plants.

SCORE 1 if there is only one variety of vegetation in your garden.

SCORE 1 if the vegetation in your yard is not indigenous to the area.

SCORE 2 for a garden or lawn without paths.

SCORE 2 for a garden or yard without seating.

The total negative score could be 8. Naturally, curing all negative conditions is the ideal to strive toward. If you have scored almost one half of the total score, consider it a warning signal and attend to making some changes as soon as possible. Being surrounded by the best conditions helps you thrive!

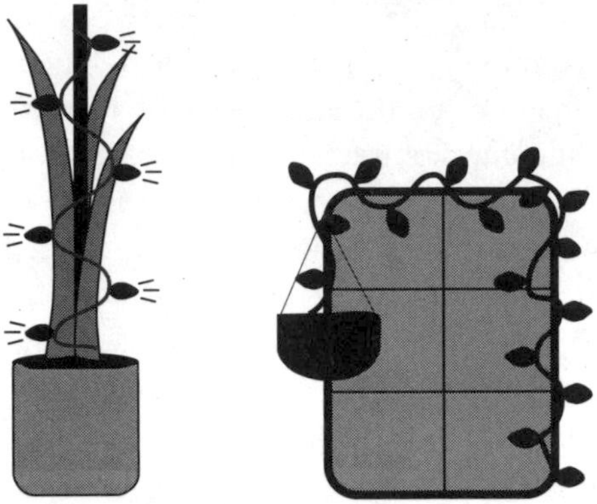

Cures to increase the benefits of solitary houseplants

If you do not have any houseplants . . .

Evolutionary psychologists now believe that humans are genetically programmed to engage in behavior that will advance their gene pool into the next generation. Because our offspring require a longer period of care than those of any other mammal, we need to have a natural predisposition toward long-term caregiving. We are connected to our natural biology when given an opportunity to care for living things, so caring for plants satisfies an important instinct.

Install a plant or a representation of vegetation inside your living space. If you don't possess the proverbial green thumb, ask a local nursery to sell you a hardy vine that is appropriate for your area. Train the vine to drape over a windowsill or wrap around a pole. Adding light or color increases the chi of the vignette.

Be creative and have fun. If a plant dies, be sure to get another. Also, it's better to have a silk plant than none at all. A silk plant connects us to nature in the same way a painting of a landscape does.

If your garden is without variety . . .

A black dress without a scarf or a necklace, a hat without an embellishment, or a home without an object d'art

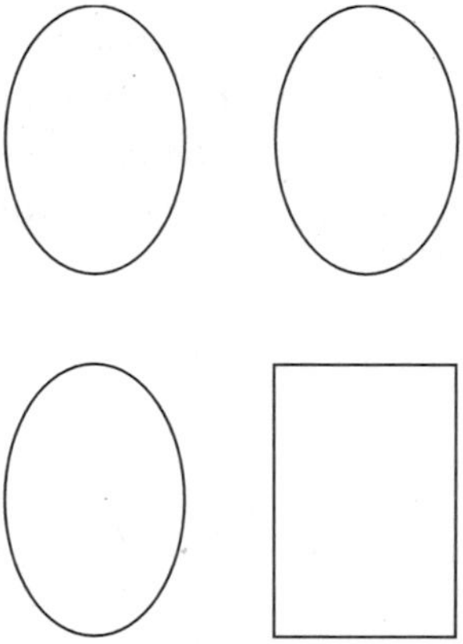

Which pair arrests the eye?

is rarely compelling. Yet we need to introduce variety in only minuscule amounts to transform the mundane into something exciting.

Just as a landscape or other view without variety can prevent us from thriving (see Chapter 9), a lawn with only grass seems lifeless next to one that includes a variety of textures, colors, and shapes. Places of extreme hardships like the Sahara Desert and the North Pole are characterized by lack of obvious variety, texture, and color. Living in a stark world seems to be synonymous with hardship.

A flowering magnolia tree, a burst of red geraniums, pines next to deciduous trees, and heather next to bamboo are all examples of variation in a yard's vegetation. A garden can feed the soul, so make yours sumptuous.

What detains the eye captures our attention. Look at the drawing of four shapes. Notice how when two ovals are placed next to each other the eye glides over both. When the rectangle is next to the oval the eye stops to consider each shape individually. Change commands attention.

When we stop the eye, we experience a space as larger. A small change can have an immense impact. Diversity delights and expands.

Even a postage stamp-size lawn can be divided into different areas. Manipulate size, color, and texture to achieve startling results. Hang wind-sensitive objects, birdhouses, or light-refracting objects like crystals from trees or poles and install a small recirculating fountain. Plant flowers not in rows but in circles and amorphous shapes to surprise the eye. Weave paths around your home. Install trellises to contain areas, and connect two poles with a string and drape vines across to give birth to a threshold.

If you are trying to maintain plants not indigenous to the climate . . .

Trying to raise plants not native to the climate or soil requires more time and care, and also more artificial supports such as the extra water and chemicals needed by the northern grasses transplanted to our Florida soil.

Adding varied detail stops the eye and creates separate areas out of one.

Maintaining a yard full of nonindigenous plants is like trying to keep a hairstyle in place while diving into a pool.

Zeroscaping is the term used for allowing only what is natural and native to decorate your vistas. I've seen the magic of a field of wildflowers grace an Ohio front lawn. I've watched in delight as sea oats and sea grapes creep over the edges of an ocean dune and consume the backyard of an oceanfront home. The land and setting are one in such cases.

The benefit of being in a place that needs no artificial intervention is similar to running a marathon in the middle of thousands of enthusiastic athletes instead of jogging down a deserted street alone. Life is easier when supported by similar surroundings.

If your garden is without a path . . .

When I am pressed against the twisted velvet ropes cordoning off rooms in historic homes, I feel frustrated and removed from the experience of what once was. I want to unhook those dividers and sneak inside. Only then will I feel as if I can know how it felt to be living in those times. Only by hands-on experience can we truly be in a moment. Denying yourself a connection to your garden is similar to leaving a room empty inside a home. It feels as if something is missing from your life.

Create a path that undulates around your property. No matter how small the parcel of land, it will feel larger with a path that twists and turns around all four sides of a property.

We reduce our awareness for any situation by reducing a vista to a single vantage point. To be able to see all sides we need to expose ourselves to the whole picture. Be sure to forge a pathway through life and your garden that leaves nothing unseen.

If there is no seating in your yard . . .

One sure way to feel formal and uncomfortable in any situation, especially in a boss's office, is not to be invited to sit down. When left standing we are always visitors, never guests. Do not be a visitor in your own world. Your yard is a room and should have an inviting place for repose.

A stump of a tree, a log rolled to a water's edge, a hammock, or a wide-top fence's rail can serve as a seat in a yard. Don't feel as if the only remedy is running out and buying outdoor furniture. An inventive mind will find solutions when spending money is not a happy option.

11

Building Sites

There is usually a best place to be, whether you're on a ticket line, in a theater, or at a racetrack's starting gate. Whether it's being in a favored position compared with others or being in a place without interference, where you are determines your experience. A home needs to be in a favored position to afford those living in it the most pleasant and beneficial experience.

I grew up in New Jersey on a street that scrambled up a mountain. The Orange Mountains spring from the earth like the back of a hippopotamus sitting in a muddy puddle of water. My childhood home was perched almost at the apex of this hump. From our front door we could see eastward toward the New York skyline. Behind our home, roots of maple and oak trees clung like fingers to the mountain's edge. My home had the advantage of being in a perfect place.

Each morning we left home facing a smiling world. The sun fell across our paths, infusing us with cheer and optimism, and below stretched a valley that was broken by a pristine Hudson River. Buffered from the northern winds by the forest and a mound of land, our house sat snug in the crevice of a mountain rise.

The time was right too. New Jersey did not have the industry that later would blight its landscape. The valley floor still had patches of green and trees between the buildings. Not every inch of my mountain was covered with houses, and there were still fields to explore. Deer didn't wreak havoc in gardens, and raccoons didn't need our garbage to live on because there was enough land to allow them to forage for food. Water was pure enough to drink from a stream on a hot summer's day, and snow remained milky white until spring, when it melted like ice cubes left too long in an unfinished drink.

My home's site infused me with a sense of safety, love of the earth, and a deep understanding that our place on this planet is as dear as a loved one. Just as easily as I flew down the hill each day toward school, later in life I would set forth to accomplish a goal.

Test

Score 2 if land ascends from a front entrance.

Score 2 for a building completely exposed, unprotected by topography or vegetation.

Score 2 for a home situated on a floodplain or too close to a noisy body of water.

Score 2 for a home situated at a T-juncture.

Score 2 for a home built too close to a noisy road.

Score 2 for a home built on a former sacred site.

Score 3 for a home built over contaminated minerals, an earthquake fault, or a strong underground stream.

The total negative score could be 15. Naturally, curing all negative conditions is the ideal to strive toward. If you have scored almost one half of the total score, consider it a warning signal and attend to making some changes as soon as possible. Being surrounded by the best conditions helps you thrive!

If the land in front of your entrance ascends . . .

Can you imagine waking up each morning and negotiating a sleepy self up a sloping kitchen floor to brew your favorite morning drink? Starting off each day facing an obstacle might, over time, make you dread getting up. In the same way, homes surrounded by ascending land wear the occupants down.

In addition, rainwater will pour down the incline, runaway vehicles could skid off the road, and mudslides might bring heaps of unwanted earth to your doorstep. It might feel as if trouble is seeking you out.

Avoid buying a home situated at the base of a hill. If you are already there, try the following:

- Plant a row of hedges or barrier vegetation at the top of an incline.
- Mount a conspicuous object such as a mailbox or a gate near the top. With an end in sight, any journey seems possible.
- If feasible, reduce the risers of the steps to four to five inches to lessen the effort required to reach the street.

If your home is exposed and unprotected by topography or vegetation . . .

While traveling in Italy, my husband and I were thrilled by castles perched atop hills dotting the Umbrian landscape. Positioned to present a strong image, these buildings were situated high above all others. Perfect for royalty; not so practical for the rest of us.

Screen your home with appropriate vegetation. Consider adding vegetation to be a finishing touch like accessorizing an outfit. Although you are dressed without it, the total appeal is enhanced by embellishments.

If you live on a high floor of an apartment building, place at least one lightweight object such as a plant or a sculpture in front of the windows. The object will command attention and redirect chi to the home's interior.

If you live on a floodplain or too close to a noisy body of water . . .

A river can flood, a tidal body of water can encroach, and a waterfall can deafen other sounds. The need to feel shielded from an uncontrollable force is as natural as seeking shelter during a hailstorm. When a property is bordered by a powerful body of water, a dwelling should be positioned away from tide or swelling flood waters and farther from any tumultuous din that can smother the sounds of human voices. Even if you do not see water, if there is a body of water in proximity to your dwelling, check to see if you are on a floodplain.

I once visited an old mill that had been transformed into a home. Because it was right next to a waterfall, the noise inside was deafening. I found my voice completely stressed out by the end of what was supposed to be a relaxing dinner party. The owners were weekenders from New York City and were more accustomed to a racket and seemed less irritated by it. Still, I wonder how much more recuperative their weekend sojourn would have been had the home been a hundred feet from the cascading waters.

Position statues, fountains, ornamental plantings or pole lights, a gazebo, or a deck between your home and the noise source. Inside, add wood furniture or earth accessories. Since the elements earth and wood absorb water, their symbols here will neutralize the imbalance.

It is not surprising that ship berths above the waterline are priced higher than those below. If your house is adjacent to a waterfall, make sure the seating is not low. Looking down at torrents of water is more comforting than seeing them above.

If your home is situated at a T-juncture . . .

Like a target for an arrow, a home at the end of a street acts as a bull's-eye for the energy rushing down that road. The house is literally standing in the middle of a roadway. Traffic shoots directly at it, making occupants feel as if they have to sidestep impending danger.

To solve this problem for my neighbor, I repositioned her entrance pathway so that it turns away from the road, planted vegetation to screen the house from the road, and mounted a light on one side to diffuse the glare of headlights by illuminating a broad area.

Traffic aims directly at a house at the end of a T-juncture.

Cures for a house at the end of a T-juncture

If your home is situated too close to a noisy road . . .

All of our visual experiences should ebb and flow as do the tides. Like watching a tornado whip by, being in a home that is close to a constant source of noise or movement can unnerve.

When a gathering space or bedroom faces a busy roadway, diminish the effects by installing high-wattage lighting across from any window with a view of the busy road. Arrange seating to face away from that view. Create a dramatic vignette compelling enough to keep attention inside. If a large, imposing focal point like a fireplace, an indoor recirculating fountain, or a huge painting is not available, cluster many smaller objects. A group of pottery bowls, a mélange of plants, or a display of collectibles can be used successfully to focus attention inside.

If your home is built on sacred ground . . .

A few years ago I received a call from a couple who had recently left my neighborhood. After they had "moved up" to a larger, grander riverfront house, the husband began to suffer a reversal of fortunes. They implored me to come over and find out why this was happening. Their address, Indian Mound Trail, was my first concern. I asked over the telephone if their home was built on an ancient Indian burial ground. Although they didn't know, they did know that a tribe of Indians had once dwelled in the area surrounding the riverbank.

As I drove there later that week, I observed swells of earth untypical in the normally flat Florida landscape. Could they be like tells, artificial rises of earth covering an old settlement? Moreover, in a landscape dotted with great old live oaks, my friends' lot was unusually bare. Later, when I asked how many trees were toppled to build their home, I was told few if any. That increased my suspicion that my former neighbors were living on the site used by a local tribe for special purposes.

Connection with the universal spirit of a place is an expression of reverence for all. Whether it's natural or a result of human intervention, we should honor what has gone on before.

The recommended cure for my former neighbors was to install a memorial on the property. I suggested building a fountain with indigenous coquina rock and using objects similar to those that might be buried underneath to decorate the site. This required research and became a joint project for parents and children. They found pictures of appropriate pottery and shell jewelry and replicated the designs on paper, which they wrapped in a box and nestled underneath the earth. While it was a lesson in humility, it also served to strengthen this family's unity.

If your home is built above powerful underground features . . .

I had a friend who discovered his home was infiltrated by deadly radon when he put it up for sale. Real estate laws protecting potential buyers required radon checks because this area was known for high levels of the harmful gas. He contracted the services of a company licensed to reduce radon levels by vacuuming out the toxic fumes below the foundation. Although not cheap, this procedure can mitigate life-threatening problems caused by radon gas.

Unfortunately, he had not taken care to provide this benefit to himself and his family. A short time later he, a nonsmoker, developed lung cancer and died. It was agreed by medical experts that two decades of living in a home with toxic levels of radon might have caused his condition. Take the time to ascertain conditions under the earth in your area and don't delay taking the necessary measures to remedy them.

If a home is near earthquake activity, build with strong material, and place the sleeping area away from overhead beams, shelves, and high cabinets. If well water is contaminated, filter it.

12

The Pathway to a Home

It has often been said that anticipation is better than realization. Just as an hors d'oeuvre piques your appetite for the meal to come, a pathway heightens anticipation for what you're about to experience inside.

How you arrive at your doorstep each day makes a difference. Compare opening a birthday present wrapped in colorful tissue paper with opening one rolled up in newspaper. Walking a path to your front door should evoke an internal sigh of relief, for you should feel relaxed and deeply safe and secure as you step onto the familiar ground that is home.

Most houses are visible from the street, while apartments are entered from a communal hallway. A pathway creates the transition from public to private space and begins defining a home territory. Define this space through color, texture, or variety of vegetation. Distinctive plantings, unique pathway materials, and a particular shape of flower bed might be the only distinctions between your home and the next. If you live in an apartment, you can distinguish your front door from the neighbors' by hanging an appropriate symbol or placing a decorative rug at the threshold.

Test

Score 2 if there is no discernible path to an entrance door.

SCORE 1 if a home is frequently entered from a garage.

SCORE 2 if the pathway is straight.

SCORE 1 if there are no visual diversions along the path.

SCORE 1 if the door to the home cannot be seen from the beginning of the path.

The total negative score could be 7. Naturally, curing all negative conditions is the ideal to strive toward. If you have scored almost one half of the total score, consider it a warning signal and attend to making some changes as soon as possible. Being surrounded by the best conditions helps you thrive!

If there is no pathway to your front door . . .

Having no pathway to an entrance door can make you feel unwanted or unwelcomed. Whether it is hand-cut slate or grass trampled by use, a guide to the front door welcomes you home.

Although we think of a path as a walkway that traverses a physical distance, the transition between the outside world and inside home can be achieved in other ways. A pathway can be created when the eye is halted and impelled to look at an object before moving on. Even apartment dwellers who live with long featureless hallways can pay attention to small details along the way. Even glancing at a few favorite doormats in front of neighbors' doors can help distinguish your pathway home. If you do nothing else, hang an ornament on your door to frame a greeting.

If you often enter your home from the garage . . .

Entering a home from a garage can make you feel as if you are going through a work area. Utility rooms and kitchens, often accessed through the garage, will remind you of things you need to do or that you left undone. It is far better to enter a space that cheers and relaxes.

If it seems unlikely that you will start entering your home through its designated front entrance, hang a picture on a garage wall near the door leading in. Mount a string of lights leading to the door. Block a water heater or a pile of boxes with a screen. Clean up the garage and conceal utility items behind a curtain or a cabinet. Treat the garage entrance no differently than you would a front foyer by hanging paintings or posters, placing a vase of flowers, painting the walls a color coordinated with the rest of the home or selecting an area carpet adjacent to the door that does not reek of utility. Make sure the lighting is bright and keep it tidy. Simply painting a garage door a bright, cheerful color could suggest more of a welcome home.

If your pathway is perfectly straight . . .

Who needs to rush home or feel rushed? Science tells us that the straighter and narrower a river's bed, the

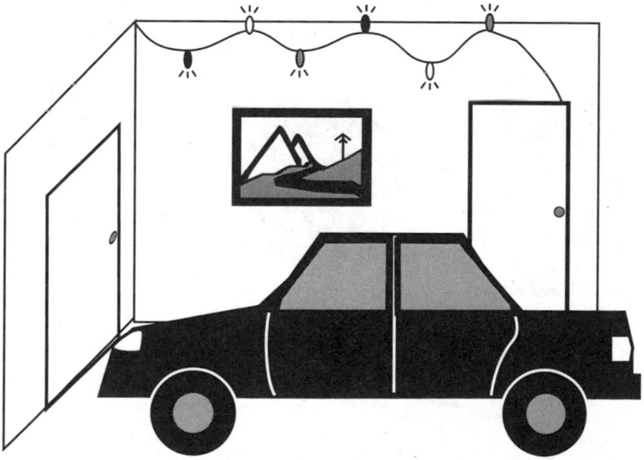

Cures for entering a home through the garage

faster the water will flow. Curved lines lead us gently, while straight lines make us rush.

Sometimes the easiest way to bend a straight path is to adjust its surroundings. For example, if you have a straight cement or brick pathway through a lawn, carve out additional lawn to restructure the path's overall shape. It can be filled with the same material as the existing pathway or decorated with plants or objects. In any case, the redistribution of materials will give a straight path the look of a curved one.

Change a straight pathway by carving out additional lawn.

When the path itself cannot be physically altered, objects on the path can force a person to move in a slower curved direction. Place a birdbath, a potted plant, or any deco-

Another way to cure a straight pathway is to place objects along it.

rative object on it. It fills in the straight line and forces a person to change direction.

If there are no visual diversions along the path . . .

The space in front of a home is its first impression. Its style, care, and adornments are initial personal indicators of the family or families inside. Put a piece of yourself into this setting. Plant flowers that reflect your favorite color, cultivate a seedling into a mature specimen, or find an object that expresses your individuality.

Even apartment dwellers, who may not have the authority to make changes in their lobby, would do well to adorn their hallway with some distinctive features. If you do no more than mount a particularly pleasing ornament on your door, you will have created a better transition into your personal world.

If you cannot see an entrance door from the beginning of the approach to a home . . .

Although trails through parks and forests are intriguing in part because where they lead is often unknown, the pathway to a home needs both to feel familiar and to reveal its destination. In Stephen R. Covey's bestselling book *Seven Habits of Highly Effective People*, one of the first rules for success is to visualize the goal and then take steps to reach it. Without the end in sight, we are not as focused and may feel more adrift. Seeing our home's entrance door revealed at the end of a pathway gives us the comfort of knowing we have reached our haven.

When I lived in New Jersey, the front door of my home faced the best direction, but not the entrance path. I positioned a mirror on a wall outside to reflect the door as I approached. The mirror served a dual purpose because when I was inside it reflected those who were

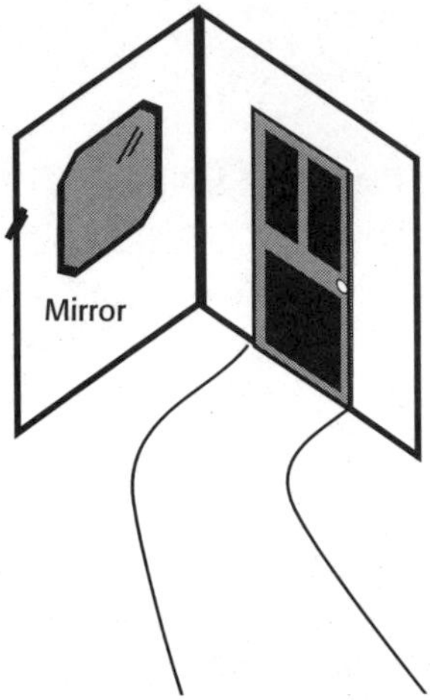

Position a mirror so an entrance door can be seen from the path.

walking up the path. When I looked out the door, I saw their image as they saw mine.

If a mirror is not a viable solution, position an object that indicates that a door may be nearby. A light, a basket of flowers, an old-fashioned shoe scraper, or even a strategically positioned wind chime could be the harbinger of the path's end.

13

The Entrance of a Home

Nothing is stronger than first impressions. For good or bad, an initial perception remains etched in our memories.

Just as the eyes mirror the soul, a front entrance reflects the combined essences residing inside. What does it communicate about you and your family? How does the area welcome and provide clues to the identity of those inside? If your door could be transplanted to a motel room, it's time to make changes. An entrance should captivate and excite people to proceed.

Test

Score 1 each if a kitchen, bathroom, or bedroom can be seen when entering a home.

Score 2 if you face a wall within eight feet after entering.

Score 2 if you enter a foyer with two views, one of a nearby wall and one of a distant room or hallway.

Score 2 if a mirror cuts off an image of any family member.

Score 1 if there is no resting surface for gloves, hat, or package near the front door.

SCORE 2 if fewer than two people can comfortably stand near the door.

SCORE 1 if an exit door is directly across from the entrance door.

SCORE 1 if a staircase is directly in front of an entrance door.

SCORE 1 if there are two staircases, one going up and one going down.

SCORE 1 if the area is dimly lit.

The total negative score could be 15. Naturally, curing all negative conditions is the ideal to strive toward. If you have scored almost one half of the total score, consider it a warning signal and attend to making some changes as soon as possible. Being surrounded by the best conditions helps you thrive!

If a bedroom, or bathroom, or kitchen can be seen upon entering . . .

More often than not, bedrooms are used for noncommunal activities. When people enter a home, all eyes should light on the home's heart or shared territory, not areas that will draw members into solo activities. Noticing a bedroom's door ajar when first entering a home can entice the bedroom's occupant to enter this space, thereby becoming separated from the communal living areas. Isolation, over the long haul, can lead to divisiveness in a family unit.

Bathrooms, designed for private functions, are also best out of a central view.

Although kitchens are central to life's fulfillment, they can consume free time. Except for people who consider cooking relaxing and creative, kitchens are work areas. We need not be reminded of kitchen labor when we enter our abode.

An entrance should make you smile, make you feel safe, and entice you to proceed to the heart of a space.

- Divert attention away from inappropriate views through the use of color, wind-sensitive objects, or light.
- Keep doors to bedrooms, bathrooms, and kitchens closed.
- Position substantial, enticing objects to lure attention away from those rooms. For example, a bookcase positioned to the far side of a door can conjure up pleasures of reading. Photographs of family members can be a magnet for interest.
- A pool of light or a wall with a high-intensity color can channel attention to the heart of a home.

If a wall blocks a view inside upon entering . . .

When we mentally come to a blank wall, we experience the discomfort of having our thoughts thwarted, knocked off track, or constrained. No one likes forgetting a piece of information.

In the same way, viewing a wall when entering a home stymies our progress. Our chi is stopped in its tracks. Day after day we can feel as if we are walking into a wall if it is our first sight.

Hang a mirror on the offending wall. This minimizes the wall's presence. If a mirror seems inappropriate, enchant the eye by placing flowers, plants, photos, or unusual fabrics on the wall or on nearby furniture to divert attention from the wall. A photograph of family members engaged in an activity is a good diversion because it is hard to resist looking at ourselves.

If a wall partially covers up a view into the rest of the space (split-eye) . . .

A split-eye is seeing a short view of a wall with one eye and long view with the other. An unbalanced depth in a visual field can strain the optic nerve, causing what the ancients called a *split-eye*. Since the optic nerve carries visual impulses to the brain, seeing both a close and a distant view gives a mixed message. Headaches, a feeling of imbalance, and a propensity to feel irritable can be the result of a split view.

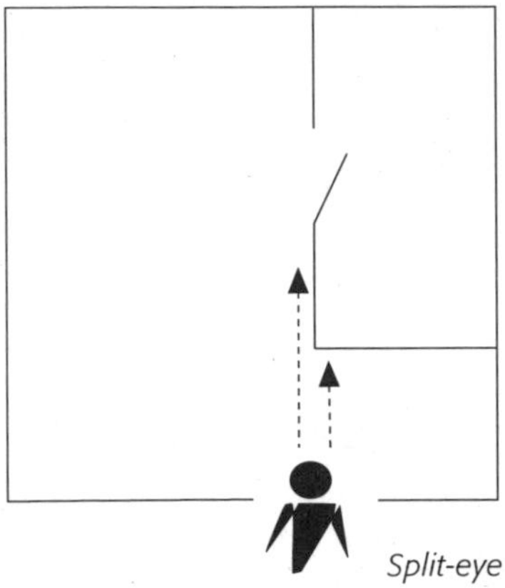

Split-eye

Place chi-stopping items that anchor the eye to either the short or long view. Just like a friend recognized in a crowd, this object should attract the eye. A plant, a sculpture, a screen, or any creative solution can do the trick.

A chi-stopping item will anchor the eye to the short or long view, curing split-eye.

If a mirror cuts off a full view of anyone entering . . .

A mirror should not cut off the reflection of those entering.

Samuel, the artist who illustrated this book, is six feet, six inches tall. He finds his head cut off visually by mirrors in most front foyers because they are hung to accommodate the average adult's height. A mirror that does not reflect an entire image is negative. Either for tall adults or for children, a severed image communicates that you are not considered important enough to see. So hang a mirror at eye level for all family members.

When my son Zachary topped six feet, four inches, I repositioned a bathroom mirror so that he would not feel as if he were being pushed out of the house by his disappearing image. Be sensitive to the small and tall members of your world and how they experience themselves in reflective surfaces around a home.

If your entrance has a foyer without a surface on which to rest objects . . .

Traditional feng shui considers the area to the right of a door the "helpful people corner," while the pyramid school considers it the compassion area. When you provide a place on which to rest objects or be leaned on for physical or emotional support, you are expressing compassion for the needs of others. Life is a circle, and the concern you display for others ultimately returns to you.

Any surface on which a hand can rest, no matter how small, will do. An umbrella stand and a converted antique ashtray are alternatives to a table or shelf. If no floor space exists, a wall sconce can serve as a space indicator and highlight your compassion for others.

If you have a small, constraining entrance foyer . . .

A small entrance can be likened to a tight belt: it constricts. Few of us are comfortable being in a crush of people crowding a theater's exit to leave. Having an appropriate amount of space surrounding an entrance or exit is imperative to good feng shui.

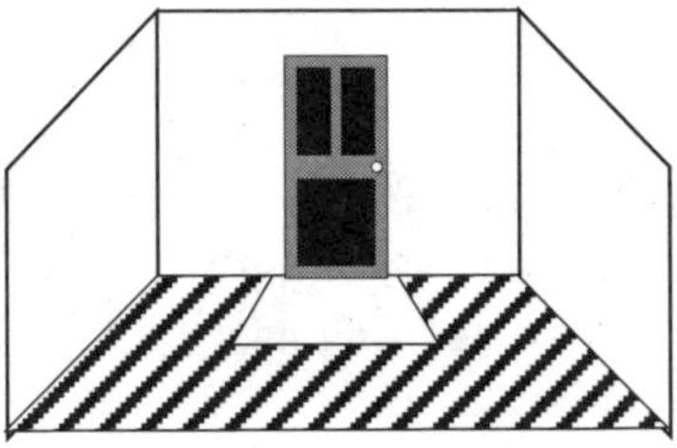

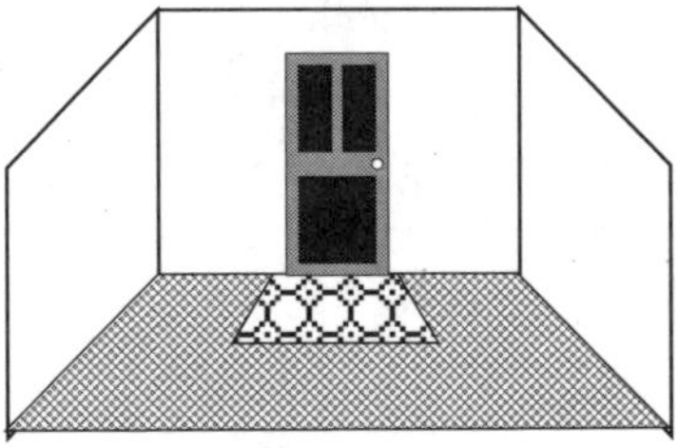

Varying flooring can expand a foyer.

When the actual square footage doesn't permit a spacious entrance, you can fool the eye by varying flooring materials. Carve a hunk out of wall-to-wall carpet and insert a flooring with a different texture, pattern, or color or throw an area carpet over the existing surface. A change of flooring can alter your perception of space.

If there is an entrance door facing an exit door or a window . . .

When I visited India, I was confused by the left-to-right gesture of the head while the mouth uttered yes. In a similar way, an exit door or window in direct view of an entrance door is saying "Come right in" while showing you where to leave or attracting your attention outside. The Chinese would explain that our energy or chi is pulled through the existing space or lured to looking at what's beyond. We are inclined to follow where we are visually led and if not distracted are likely to continue on to the end.

Provide a distraction to divert attention from an exit path. A pool of light, a change in flooring, or a physical object can deflect a feeling of being tempted to leave the room. A mirror positioned to catch the reflection of the person who enters or the movement of the entrance door opening can help retain our attention.

A staircase that greets people entering a home draws them up the stairs.

If a staircase is directly in front of a home's entrance . . .

A stairway in front of a door is as enticing as an escalator is to a child—almost irresistible. We are pulled to climb any stairway in view.

Because I grew up in a home where a staircase was directly

across from the main entrance, I recently asked my mother what happened when my sister and I returned home from school each day. "You went upstairs to your rooms" was her reply, confirming the theory that a staircase in line with an entrance door will propel those entering upstairs.

More often than not, the upper floor houses the private spaces, like bedrooms. The entrance to a home should prompt all to enter the heart of a home, the places commonly used by all members.

Divert attention away from the stairs with a brighter, lighter, larger object adjacent to the stairs. Install higher-wattage bulbs in the adjacent hallway. Place a bright, patterned area rug in the space leading toward the gathering spaces.

A plant, sculpture, or furniture can be positioned in such a way to provide an obstacle around which to traverse. Even if the obstacle turns us one inch, that inch, when extended out to the end of the space, will lead the eye a great distance across a room.

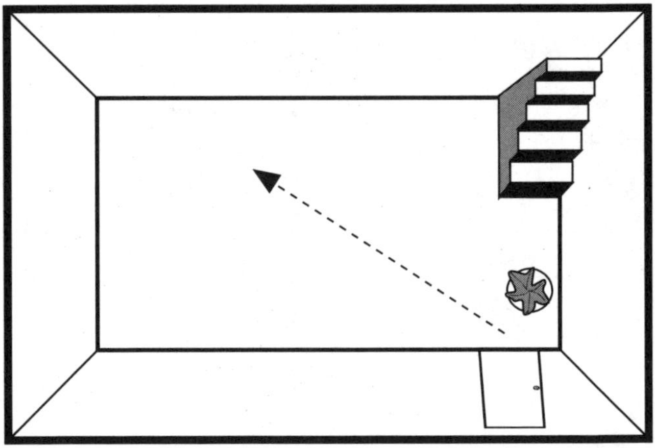

To cure a staircase across from an entrance, place a plant or other object to direct those who enter toward the heart of a space.

Try this: Stand up and look ahead. Now turn one inch and notice how far your eye has traveled across the distant vista. The eye is moved dramatically by even the lightest rotation.

If your home has a split-level entrance with one staircase going up and another going down . . .

Entering a home with a split staircase makes us feel like the sheriff in the old Laurel and Hardy skits. When the sheriff asked where a bandit went, Laurel and Hardy replied in unison, "He went that-a-way!" as they pointed in opposite directions.

When we cannot make structural changes, the remedy lies in attracting the eye to the favored spot. In this case, the level on which the main gathering room is situated is the area to highlight. Solutions might include highlighting the appropriate staircase by wrapping a string of lights around the banister, mounting a strip of lights above the baseboard, painting the ceiling above with circles of contrasting color, or painting each step a slightly different tone.

In my New Jersey home I turned an otherwise ordinary staircase into an enjoyable experience by painting the risers and treads differently and stenciling tiny messages like "You have just burned off ten calories" or "She who scrambles rises" to entertain as one ascends or descends.

Another idea is to paint the stairway wall leading to the main areas a brighter color than the wall of the less important stairway. Adorn the wall of the staircase leading to the heart of the home with paintings, posters, or three-dimensional art. Create an energy surrounding the preferred staircase to attract the eye of those who enter.

If your entrance is dimly lit . . .

The older we get, the more dependent are we on light to define our surroundings. The real and implied value of lighting should be considered carefully as the percentage of our population over fifty swells.

Bright light cheers. It is experienced as friendly and energizes our spirit. We tend to follow the light metaphorically and actually. Although a home's entrance is one area in which we spend little time, using bright light helps propel us forward toward the heart of a home.

Sometimes changing a lightbulb from sixty to one hundred watts will do the trick. Otherwise, invest in a lamp, a wall sconce, or track spotlights to brighten an entrance.

If an entrance is used almost exclusively for company, consider reversing this effect. When we are guests, we desire less light until we feel at home.

14

Secret Arrows

Secret arrows are small disturbances that, over time, have a profound impact. The easiest way to think of secret arrows is as lines of negative energy or negative chi that, while not always overt, can, like the tags sewed on the inside of an article of clothing, irritate over time. Suppose every morning a colleague who would love to have your job glares at you when you arrive at work. Over time what was at first easily ignored becomes a thorn in your side. To avoid this glance, you begin coming in earlier than usual, but that doesn't help you dodge the grimace later in the day. After a while you escape to your office and don't come out to chat with co-workers or have lunch in the cafeteria quite as much as you used to.

Your fellow workers take umbrage at your lack of attention, and soon you find yourself out of the loop, the only one who doesn't know that someone from headquarters will be making a surprise visit during the next week. The day comes, and everyone but you is ready to show his stuff. Later that year, when raises and promotions are considered, you are overlooked. Secret arrows undermine resolve and can wear down your best intentions.

In a building a secret arrow is formed by a corner or an extraordinarily large object pointing at a home or place of repose. It is easy to recognize if you know what

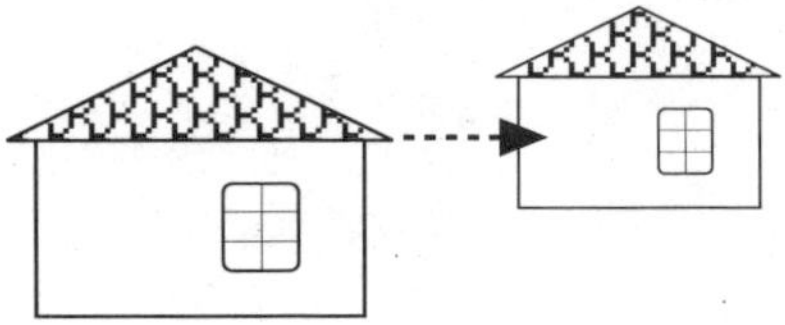

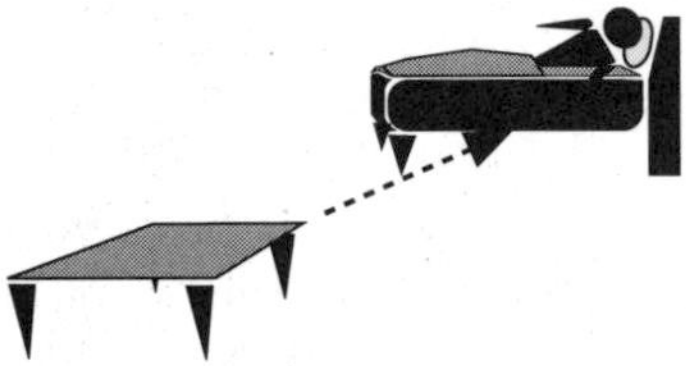

Secret arrows

to look for. Angles or arrows are formed when two lines converge, and their projectile can be physically damaging. It's painful to bump into a table corner, less so to hit something broadside. In the same way, a corner can injure your psychological health.

Secret arrows can be formed by buildings, light posts, signs, streets, roof lines, furniture, or vegetation pointing at a house. The object pointed to is normally stationary, such as a house, exit door, bed, or desk.

A secret arrow is like having a stick stuck in your side: not only can it by annoying, but eventually it can also cause harm. A positive spirit can be modified by insidious or subtle pressure.

Facing a building's edge can be compared to looking directly at a knife's sharpened point instead of at its flat harmless side. The suggestion of a cutting edge facing you as you look out a window, leave the entrance of your home, or relax in your bed or chair or at your desk can, over time, create a subconsciously negative energy. The length of time you are subjected to the arrow or the frequency of its occurrence (for example a secret arrow pointing at a desk you sit in most of the day) is an important consideration.

Test

Score 2 for each if a large building, billboard, or electrical pole looms over your home.

Score 2 for each if the edge of a roof or billboard or the corner of a building points in the direction of your home.

Score 2 for each if a wall beam or corner of another room projects into a room and its edge points at a couch, chair, or bed.

Score 2 for each if the edge of a desk or another stationary object in a home or office points at a sleeping or seating area.

There is no limit to this test's scoring. If you have more than two arrows pointed at you or at your home, it is best to correct them. You can survive with a secret arrow, but it is easier to live without them.

If your home has a building looming over it . . .

There is an expression about not living in someone's shadow that reminds us not to let another's presence overwhelm us. Like people, buildings can throw shadows and dim others nearby.

Toronto is built on the edge of Lake Ontario. The lake side used to be a safe place to stroll and spend a lovely Sunday afternoon. The original development around the lake was low in density and building size. Ultimately the water's edge became a prime development area. Huge multistoried buildings replaced the early smaller ones, and their gigantic shadows cast an ominous gloom on the surrounding area. What was once a safe place became unsafe as shadows created dark areas and places to avoid. Without sunlight, walkways became colder in winter, when sunshine makes a dramatic difference. The secret arrows cast by the larger buildings might have influenced not only the individual lives of those living and working there but also the gestalt of the entire area.

Large looming objects near your home can diminish a personal sense of well-being merely by their bulk and size. I remember sprinting to the basketball court to celebrate my son's high school team's victory. Walking among the players, I felt uncomfortable, like a sapling in a redwood forest. In the same way, we can feel overpowered by taller, bulkier buildings looming over ours.

If a large building looms over yours, put up a flagpole, hang a wind sock, increase outdoor lighting fixtures, or create a larger-than-life ornament to strengthen your home's presence. Plant vegetation to block the view, or hang a bell or wall chime on your door to create a frenzy of energy as you open it.

If a corner of a building, billboard, or other large object is pointed at your home . . .

An object doesn't have to be larger than a home and looming over it to affect you negatively. Objects positioned ominously can pluck away your share of good fortune.

Since moving a building is rarely an option, you must find another way to reduce the negative impact of an arrow. Chapter 5 explained how different materials (fire, earth, metal, water, wood) can reduce the potency of others. This is a perfect time to apply this knowledge.

For example, if a roof's corner points at a front door, ascertain what the shingles are made of. If asphalt (made from both earth and metal elements) you can use water in your cure, since that is the element that reduces both earth and metal. Placing real water or its symbol, such as a birdbath, a recirculating fountain, a mirror, or any black or blue object such as a black scalloped piece of paper between the roof's corner and your front door will undermine or reduce the potency of the negative arrow formed by the shingles.

If a corner of another room or wall beam is directed at a sitting or sleeping area . . .

Have you ever been alone and for no discernible reason suddenly had the annoying feeling that someone was staring at you? This may happen when corners or wall beams are directed at the place where you are sitting or sleeping.

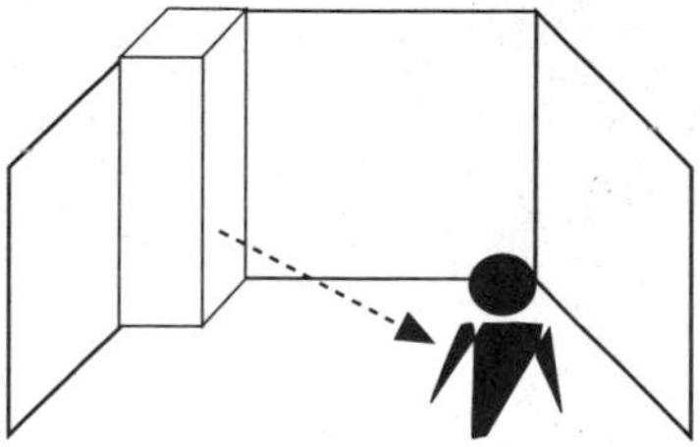

Watch out for corners of walls that point at sitting or sleeping areas.

Reposition important seating and sleeping areas away from the line extending from the corner. If this is impossible, place a small table, lamp, plant, or sculpture next to the furniture affected by the arrow to block the impact. If the object is made of an element that will reduce the element of the secret arrow, you will double the effect of your remedy. Since plaster is composed of the earth element and wood absorbs the nutrients from earth, thereby reducing its vitality, a wood table next to a bed would mitigate a wall beam's effect.

If the edge of a desk or another object in a home or office is pointed at a sleeping or seating area . . .

Having the edge of a desk, cabinet, or table directed at you feels the same as having a finger pointed in your direction. Here are some ways to lessen the annoyance of a secret arrow:

- If the arrow is formed by wood furniture, place a ceramic planter with plant facing the arrow. Earth eventually wears down (rots) wood.
- If the arrow is formed by furniture with a triangular cornice or cabinet painted red, place a vase of water facing the arrow to put out the flame.
- If the arrow is formed by metal furniture, place a vase of flowers on the furniture that receives the arrow. Water rusts metal.
- If the arrow is formed by a glass-topped table, position an article made of wood to block the arrow. Wood absorbs water, and glass represents the element water.

15

The Neighborhood

Before superhighways whipped across America and airplane routes were as heavily trafficked as Main Street, USA, neighborhoods were our second skin. We knew who lived in the homes that dotted our streets. We were known by the merchants as well as the moms and pops who spent their leisure time on their porches or backyards. In short, we lived in a world that stayed familiar.

Unlike other species, we are able to modify our surroundings to stretch the borders of our lives. It is not enough to be fed sufficiently and housed securely. We humans have doggedly searched for new ways to minimize our need for the art of survival and maximize the experience of pleasure and leisure. In doing so we sometimes overlook the fact that our empowerment lies in a feeling of connection to family and community.

A neighborhood has a personality much as an individual does. Taste, as well as social and economic conditions, reflects into our lives much as a mirror reflects an image. Certainly there are those who overcome the disadvantages of living within a diseased social structure, but for the most part our lives reflect our extended surroundings.

I could no more live in a neighborhood with uniform, manicured lawns than a fish could live without water. Instead I choose to live in an eclectic neighborhood where individualism is stamped on every parcel of land. Being enveloped in a unique environment reinforces my desire to discover my own special qualities.

There is a finite number of people who can live together and consider themselves a unit. There is an ideal size for a classroom, town, state, or nation, but suburban/urban sprawl has begun to challenge human cohesiveness. Neighborhoods are our last defense in preserving a quality of life that is sustaining and meaningful.

Many of us can remember our first day at a new school. Knowing no one and being unfamiliar with the environment, some may have felt as I did—isolated in an invisible shell. Suddenly a happy coincidence! I might have dropped something on the floor and someone helped me to retrieve it or I caught a smile on a classmate's face and we sat down together to eat lunch. A connection was made and isolation vanished. To feel safe, noticed, and cared for is what ultimately bonds us to place.

Know that the word *neighbor* can mean friend, associate, companion, colleague, and mate.

TEST

SCORE 2 if there are no footpaths connecting home to home.

SCORE 1 if there is unsightly construction in your neighborhood.

SCORE 1 if there are no edges between lots, either artificial or natural (fences or trees).

SCORE 1 if there is no community gathering point in the neighborhood, either commercial or informal.

Score 2 if your home or a building in direct view of your home has no windows facing the street.

Score 2 if you are feuding with any neighbor.

The total negative score could be 9. Naturally, curing all negative conditions is the ideal to strive toward. If you have scored almost one half of the total score, consider it a warning signal and attend to making some changes as soon as possible. Be surrounded by the best conditions to help you thrive!

If there are no footpaths connecting homes in a neighborhood . . .

Sidewalks are the veins of a neighborhood, connecting home to home and street to street. By providing safe passageways as well as definable routes, sidewalks keep a landscape peopled. It is nourishing to live in a place punctuated with a measure of activity.

The sidewalks are the common ground for individuals to become members of a larger household. Whether for play, strolls, or social intercourse, sidewalks provide a forum for connection.

Not long ago I read a glowing obituary for William Levitt, founder and builder of Levittown, an early suburban development on Long Island, New York. After World War II, to accommodate those who wanted to flee the cities, Levitt erected homes in the same way as Henry Ford manufactured automobiles. With assembly-line production concepts he streamlined construction techniques and produced affordable mass housing. Although this is a noble idea, I am enraged by his methods.

I could only grudgingly forgive his razing the natural topography, cropping hills, and filling in valleys so his road-building equipment would have the smallest area to prepare and surface.

I can somewhat understand uprooting trees and other vegetation that would restrict direct access to a building site. Dragging building materials by hand would add to a home's expense.

Carving out similar building lot shapes and sizes would give the neighborhood a feeling of equality, somewhat like the human race having identical genetic composition. Identical layouts could be mitigated by inventiveness and imagination. Perhaps the carbon-copy look would propel families to invent, originate, and procure a uniqueness of space.

However, the last straw, the final blow to the inhabitants of this new city, was the elimination of sidewalks and a mix of residential and commercial side by side. Gone was common ground for human contact.

Streets could not provide safe connecting ground as automobiles filled up these arteries. The landscape became dotted with sealed metal cells transporting the population out of the neighborhood to shop, work, and attend school. No longer was it usual to love thy neighbor as thyself; it was now unusual to know thy neighbor.

If there are no traditional sidewalks, be inventive. Carve a piece of lawn away and create a minipark on your front lawn. Some communities built without benefit of sidewalks are banding together to designate an access strip of land either in front or at the rear of properties to be used for walking, bike riding, or jogging. Build enthusiasm for a common path across backyards as a safe arena for children to ride bikes and people to stroll. I have seen paths defined by stones, flags, flowers, or just pebbles cross an expanse of green lawns. It doesn't matter what it is as long as it expresses the intent to create an appropriate common walking space within a community.

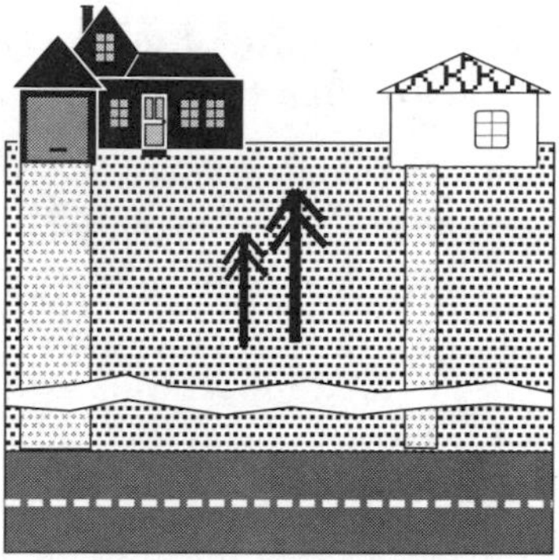

Create an access strip where no sidewalk exists.

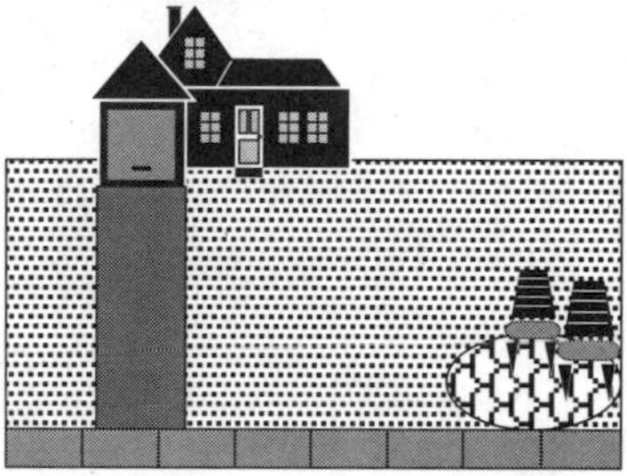

Another cure for a lack of sidewalks is to create a meeting area on one yard.

Not all will support designating their private property for this use, but communities have benefited even when dotted with dead ends. Sometimes resident families' objections crumble in the face of successful implementation.

If community consensus fails, erect a flag on your property indicating there is a meeting ground or miniplayfield on your front lawn. If you live in an apartment complex, encourage the management to provide such an area. Intention is a beginning that can forge the way to solution.

Hallways are apartments' sidewalks. Marshall a sense of community by getting to know each other. Throw a party twice a year in your lobby or hallway! List the names of new tenants near the elevator or stairwell. In some way, shape, or form, get to know one another. We rarely turn our backs on someone we know.

If there are uncared-for pockets or construction in your neighborhood . . .

If there is construction in your neighborhood, pick a new route home to avoid viewing it. Position a plant or any object that commands visual attention in front of the window that frames the offending view. If necessary, temporarily reposition seating in your home to avoid facing a view of the construction. Since construction is temporary, this is a temporary change in your living conditions; even if not ideal, it will soon be over.

Neighborhood blight is a more damaging, long-lasting condition. One spot of rust on a car's exterior will eventually erode the entire body. The dreaded cancer cell starts out as merely one in a field of billions within a body. A deteriorating situation, if not altered, can encroach into more areas of our lives than we could ever imagine. Be part of a cooperative effort to clean up any blight in your neighborhood before it impacts negatively on your life.

Tear down the borders of detachment. Be part of a team to change what could become a blight to a productive, supportive part of a neighborhood. If no one else will help, do it yourself. Think of all who will benefit by your efforts. Your self-esteem will rise with your knowledge of how your efforts will serve many.

If property perimeters are not demarcated . . .

An egg has a shell, a flower has its petals, and we have our skin to defend vital internal parts. Most living things are protected with an outer sheath. In the same way that our bodies demand privacy, so do our homes. Ancient feng shui wisdom tells us to surround our homes with a wall or fence to feel protected. We should have to reveal ourselves only when we want to.

Our homes are at the epicenter of our existence and should be safe from potential harm from the surrounding world, but in the contemporary West that need not mean removing our world from physical view. Walls and fences can further isolate our lives. Since we do not live in an extended family compound and do not have the benefit of stable communities, as existed in ancient China, it is best if we participate in the life of the community by being visually connected to it. Therefore, to honor a basic condition necessary for all creatures we must define our territory without isolating ourselves.

Edward T. Hall, in his book *The Hidden Dimension*, writes that we have biological as well as social perimeters. Even though too much or too little space can affect us negatively, what is too much is determined by social and biological conditions. For instance, an infant needs a restricted area to feel free to explore. When the distance exceeds our capacity to understand, we can become distressed. Like animals, we need to feel that our terrain is defined. We need to know where our territory of responsibility ends and another begins.

If there are walls or fences surrounding your home, be sure that you can see past this containment to the surrounding area. A beautiful tree, a particularly pleasing vista, should be seen from inside a home. You can pick and choose, but in most cases being connected with life in a neighborhood is beneficial.

Use vegetation, like a stand of trees, a row of flowers, or vines climbing up a trellis, to clarify boundaries without obliterating views.

If you live in a neighborhood without a commercial or informal gathering area . . .

Just as a home without a gathering room would seem ridiculous, a neighborhood without a place to congregate is absurd. Even so, many communities are built without this feature.

When a suburbanite needs milk, getting it is no longer as simple as sending a child down the street to fetch it. These days families usually must drive to gather their supplies. In the process they miss many opportunities to meet as they traverse the distance in isolation.

In my current neighborhood, we have designated one neighbor's driveway as a meeting place. The family's garage has been transformed into a gym, with various neighbors contributing different pieces of fitness equipment. Every evening the door flings open and whoever wants to can enter for conversation or exercise. It provides for a pleasant interlude and transforms a group of homes into a neighborhood.

My parents moved into their present Florida condominium and loved it from day one. The lobby, an epicenter of condominium social life, had a bulletin board listing activities. Elevators became centers for social chitchat, and the subsequent walk to the front door a time to greet neighbors who happened to be in the hallway. All in all this mix of neighborhood and social community gave them a sense of belonging that they would have otherwise lacked if they had moved to a sidewalkless single-family Florida neighborhood.

Discover a comfortable place to gather in your neighborhood. It may be by the school bus stop in the morning. It may be part of the lawn mowing ritual on a weekend afternoon, or at a community holiday party once a year. In any case, a traditional event can make the difference between anonymity and connection.

If your home has no windows facing the street or if from your home you can see a building with no windows . . .

In the same way as an individual needs to be connected, a community needs threads that weave all the parts together. Jane Jacobs, the social theorist whose ideas gave rise to many city planning considerations, deemed "eyes on the street" an essential ingredient in the safety, effectiveness, and spirit of a community. Without windows facing shared areas, a community will have no guardians.

Whether it's the street, park, alleyway, or road, some view to the neighborhood is essential. A mirror pointed in the right direction can reflect a hidden view. Invent ways to position mirrors to reflect views.

Position a reading chair, a workstation, or a breakfast table to look out over some view of your neighborhood. As I write this book, I feel less sequestered because my desk looks onto the front of my home. Schoolchildren leaving each morning, surfers carrying their boards to the beach, walkers, and joggers all are a pleasant interlude from staring at my monitor, trying to conjure up the best ways to write this book.

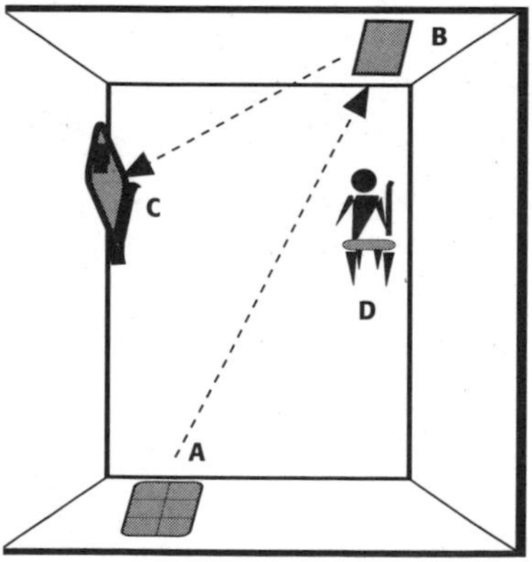

Mirror reflecting mirror to allow a view of the street:

A. Window with view of outside

B. Mirror reflecting view

C. Mirror reflecting mirror reflecting view

D. Person in chair looking at mirror reflecting mirror reflecting window and view

Curing a view of a building with no windows is more difficult. The best we can do in most cases is reinforce our own connection options. Position a telephone, TV, or radio next to a window that faces a building with no eyes on the street.

If there are negative feelings between you and neighbors . . .

Although ill health does not jump to mind when you think about not getting along with neighbors, it may be an undesired result. I know a person who curtailed her fair-weather after-dinner walk because she did not want to pass the home of a family with whom she was feuding. Ultimately she gained weight due to a reduction in exercise, which caused her blood pressure to soar. Her unhealthy condition was in truth caused by the trouble she was having with her neighbors.

Our immune system, the guardian of our health, responds to human emotions. Happiness, laughter, and joy have been proven not only to maintain well-being but also to cure illness. Norman Cousins in his book *Anatomy of an Illness* helped to cure a connective tissue disease by inundating his life with movies, books, and friends that could make him laugh.

Whatever the neighbor did, let it go. Is holding a grudge worth the demise of your health, spirit, or joie de vivre? Probably not. Focusing on the positive, not the negative, is a way of creating abundance for yourself. Let the universal law deal with your neighbor. Rise above negativity and enjoy the fruits of positive behavior, which include health, happiness, and success.

The Cures

Architectural Details

16

The Shape of a Home

Nature keeps adjusting the shape of a species until there is a perfect union between survival and form. When form does not follow function, form becomes antiquated.

There are inherently best shapes to support certain functions. And *function* is defined not only by the physical conditions of being but also by cultural prerogatives.

To determine a shape for the container in which we live or work, we need first to understand the local topography, climate, culture, and social conditions. If land is mountainous and steep, the shape may be limited to one with steps or multiple stories to provide adequate square footage. If the climate is cold, sleeping rooms might be designed with low ceilings for warmth. A family with children living at home might locate bedrooms differently from a family whose grown children visit as guests several times a year. Finally, considerations such as mental or physical handicaps, work spaces, and special living arrangements as in school dormitories or retirement communities must be evaluated to produce the best overall results. Individual and group needs must be separated, scrutinized, and put back together in a way that makes sense.

A good example of this would be a home with separate bedroom wings. In these homes children's and parents' bedrooms are positioned at opposite ends. Separating children from guardians who are responsible for their care is about as clever as allowing a child to wander in a department store alone. You aren't guaranteeing they'll be lost, but certainly the odds are increased that they will. A good layout will support each individual as well as the intention of the group.

TEST

SCORE 2 for each bedroom, kitchen, or gathering room that juts out from the main shape of a home.

SCORE 1 if you have a U-shaped home and live in a cold climate.

SCORE 1 if the upper floors overhang the lower levels.

SCORE 1 if a home has too many angles and levels.

SCORE 2 if the longer sides of a rectangle are more than three and a half times the shorter sides.

The total negative score could be 7. Naturally, curing all negative conditions is the ideal to strive toward. If you have scored almost one half of the total score, consider it a warning signal and attend to making some changes as soon as possible. Be surrounded by the best conditions to help you thrive!

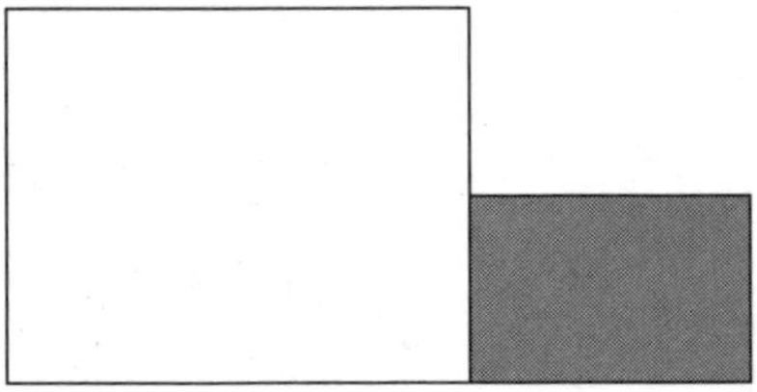

A protruding room is inauspicious in some cases.

If your home has a room protruding from the main shape of a house . . .

Whatever activity takes place in a room that is outside of the main frame of the home will feel diminished and unattached. If the room is a bedroom, an occupant may not feel nurtured by the bosom of family life. It's a feeling akin to being picked last for a volleyball team. You are on the team, but your status is minimal because you are selected last.

The family structure in ancient China varied little from decade to decade. Most homes sheltered a nuclear and/or extended family unit. Divorce, unrelated roommates, home office, and same-sex families were as rare as a baby blue ox. For the most part, families consisted of two adults, children, and in some cases an aged parent or relative. Today living spaces should be sensitive to the needs of different configurations.

It is not unusual to find a typical American family involved in separate non-family-related activities. A Saturday may find the mother catching up on her home-based consulting firm's paperwork, the father attending a class for additional certification, a teenage daughter at rugby practice, and a ten-year-old son engrossed in a Nintendo game. We applaud diversity, and our homes must help it flourish.

In the preceding example, a room jutting out from the home's main shape would be an ideal location for the mother's office. It would provide convenience as well as solitude for concentration. As long as areas central to group living are integrated in a unified structural shape, the presence of an appendage may not be negative.

Locate activities that are not central to family life in the part of the home that juts out. Home offices, workshops, and rental units are the kinds of uses well served by being detached. What is not appropriate for such areas are children's activities, kitchens, bedrooms, and gathering rooms.

If you have a U-shaped home in a cold climate . . .

In warmer climates, when the outdoors is used frequently for family activities like dining or lounging, outdoor space becomes an integral part of the living unit. But in a cold climate, the base of the U will merely be a corridor that divides the home.

Use warm deeper colors, like reds, greens, purples, and yellow, in the part of the home connecting the wings. In most cases this section will house the common rooms, and these rich tones will draw family members together.

Flood the land inside the U with light at night. A visual connection to the other side lessens the divisiveness of the U shape in colder climates.

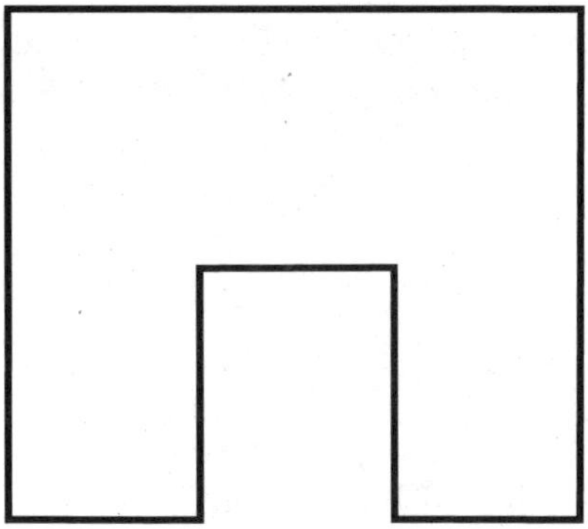

A U-shaped home is inauspicious in a cold climate.

If your home's upper floors are wider than the lower floors . . .

Like a marshmallow supported by toothpicks, a structure with upper floors broader than those below feels off balance and precarious. This configuration does not provide the visual support required to feel safe.

Plant bushes or trees or install lighting around the upper floor's perimeter, thereby lending strength to the lower floors.

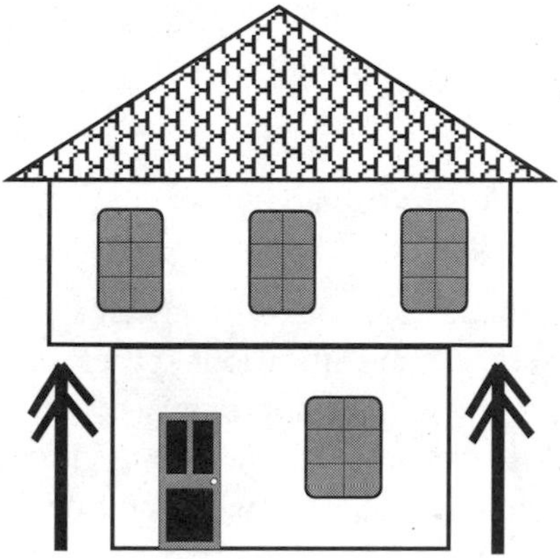

Cure for an upper floor that is wider than the lower floor

If you live in a home with too many levels and angles . . .

Distance, be it vertical or horizontal, can divide. It has been determined that a person will walk at most 1,500 feet to reach a neighborhood park. Any facility located farther away will be used infrequently.

Inside a home there are stretches that feel right. More than four levels in a home can become awkward, and more than sixty feet in any direction may be considered too far.

My cousin in San Diego lived in a modern home that hung on a mountainside. Even today, when trying to reconstruct the home in my mind, I can't come up with the number of levels. Life for her was as fragmented as her home, and marriage and her son splintered off in as many directions as the levels of the home. When she met her second husband, they quickly moved to a house that was planted firmly on the ground, and her children and marriage have been rock-solid ever since.

Cluster important rooms toward the heart of a home. Tie together the divergent areas with a connecting color theme or similar flooring or window treatments. There is something comforting and uniting in repetitive decorative schemes.

If you live in a home that has one side three and a half times longer than the other . . .

Memory of place is a term normally used to describe what contributes to feeling comfortable in various spaces. Each time we step into a house, we know approximately where everything is located. If that weren't true, we might not know where to locate a light switch or where to find the kitchen in a single-family dwelling.

Distances need to be defined through a layered evaluation system. Find the measurement between your elbow and the tips of your fingers, for example, to determine the appropriate depth of a counter space. But what is too small or too large for a home or room is less obvious. Trust your instincts. If it feels too big or if the space seems unusually ponderous to negotiate, group your main activity areas together. House activities that are less central to day-to-day living in rooms outside the core of a home.

In Roman times certain architectural standards were established that remain clearly as effective and true today as they were then. Just as people consider about 1,500 feet from their home to be their immediate neighborhood, there is a length and breadth that, when exceeded, makes a space more of an edifice and less of a home.

How big is too big? A home twenty by seventy feet is probably too long for its width. If your present dwelling feels too long in one direction, tie it together with repetitive anchors. It may be a consistent color theme throughout the entire space, a wind chime hanging at each end of the home so that a similar sound is heard throughout, or simply a repetitive flooring theme. If you keep bumping into old friends, even a huge auditorium feels friendly.

17

Doors

A door is like a lightbulb; when opened, it illuminates the whole area. On a fundamental level doors represent an escape route, and their accessibility contributes to our sense of well-being.

Doors should provide access to other areas in a way that does not disrupt a room's use. They should reveal, not conceal, the space so we feel safe when we enter or exit. Consider the irony of the old jail cell door. The bars across the front neither screen nor afford the occupant any privacy.

A door's size should match the spirit of place. It should be neither too grand for the size of the space entered, nor too small. What feels large or small enough is not a physical measurement but an emotional experience. It's right when it feels right. Where and how we enter should dissipate anxiety and elevate a positive outlook.

Test

Score 2 if there is a straight, uninterrupted path from one door to another.

Score 1 if two or more doors are in close proximity.

Score 1 if two doors facing each other are slightly out of line.

SCORE 1 for each large door opening to a small place and for each small door opening to a larger space.

SCORE 2 for each door that when opened does not lie flat against an adjoining wall.

SCORE 1 if a front door has transparent glass inserts.

SCORE 1 if an entrance door is larger or smaller in proportion to the facade of a house than a mouth is to a face.

SCORE 1 if the majority of the room cannot be seen upon entering.

The total negative score could be 10. Naturally, curing all negative conditions is the ideal to strive toward. If you have scored almost one half of the total score, consider it a warning signal and attend to making some changes as soon as possible. Correcting inauspicious conditions with doors is particularly important because as you enter, the stage is set for the experience of place. A negative encounter at the outset can alter an otherwise positive area. Being surrounded by the best conditions helps you thrive!

If your home has a straight path from one door to another . . .

A straight, uninterrupted pathway between two doors tempts us to pass through the room we've just entered. Even Alice could not refrain from opening the door to Wonderland once she tumbled down the rabbit hole. We are inclined to follow a path and, if not visually distracted, likely to continue on to the end. Fine for Alice, but not for members of our family, whom we want to encourage to linger mentally and physically in the heart

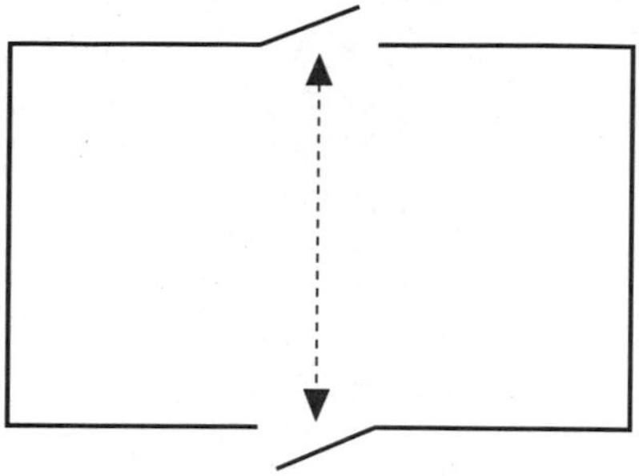

Your home should not have a straight path from one door to another.

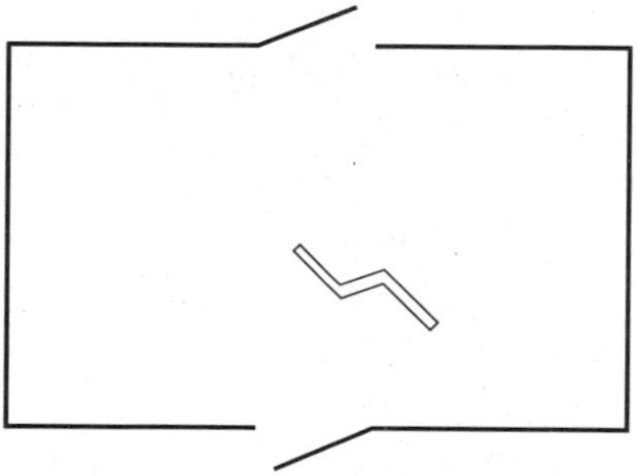

Direct the energy to the side of the home you want people to enter.

of a home. With an uninterrupted path between doors our energy or chi is propelled through the existing space and lured to what lies beyond.

Provide a distraction like a small cabinet, table, footstool, plant, sculpture, or screen that, ever so gently, repositions the person entering the space to face the area of importance in any room. If a pathway divides a room into separate areas of importance, decide which is more central and direct energy to that side. For example, in a gathering room/living room combination, it is best to direct occupants to the gathering side of the room.

If your home has two or more doors next to each other . . .

Have you ever been confronted by multiple doors after exiting an elevator? I panic in unfamiliar territory, especially when there are no reassuring signs or symbols.

Too many doors make us uncomfortable.

Even when we're familiar with the terrain and know beyond a shadow of a doubt what is behind each door, there is always a process of selection and rejection at the moment of confrontation. Too many doors in one area create tension that can provoke negativity.

If you have the luxury of building a home, make sure the doors are not crowded in one area. However, if the fates decree that you must live with multiple doors in close proximity, here's what you can do.

Provide memory clues to indicate what lies behind those doors. I am not suggesting signs like those on public toilets but rather some appropriate symbol like a sprig of dried herbs for a kitchen door, a child's current favorite idol for a bedroom door, or an infant's photograph for a nursery. Even painting the doors different colors, ones that echo the color theme of the room itself, would be enough to provide memory access for residents of the home.

If you have doors facing each other that are slightly out of line . . .

In the same way that worn tire treads ultimately affect the steering and wheel alignment in a car, doors askew can contribute to feeling unbalanced or emotionally misaligned.

Create symmetry by installing a mirror to reflect the other side. If you don't like mirrors, create a feeling of

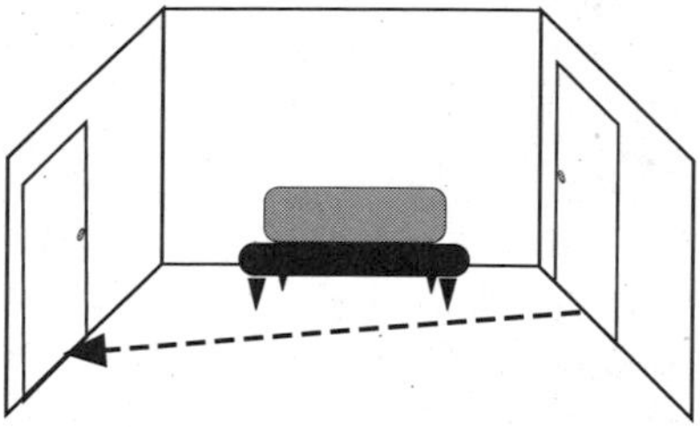

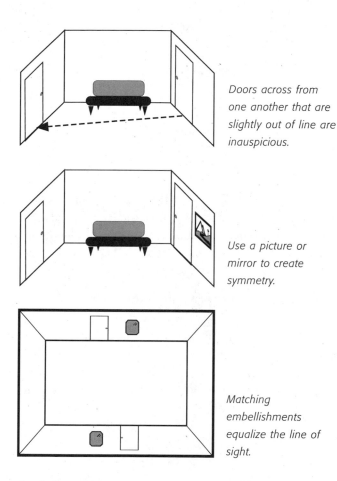

Doors across from one another that are slightly out of line are inauspicious.

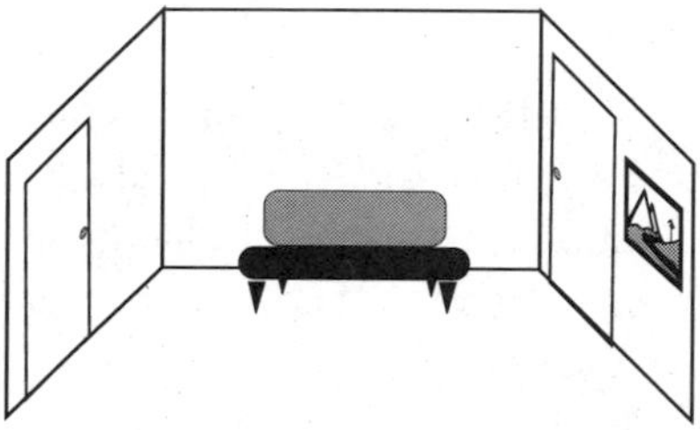

Use a picture or mirror to create symmetry.

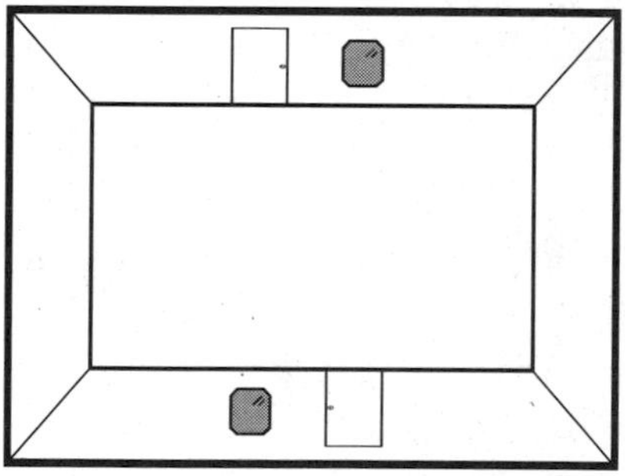

Matching embellishments equalize the line of sight.

depth by positioning an appropriate wall embellishment across from each door.

Matching wall decorations serve to equalize the line of sight and create symmetry for the soul.

If a large door or archway opens into a small area . . .

When I was growing up, one evening family ritual was to listen to my businessman father proffer pearls of wisdom. His favorite lesson was how to maintain customer loyalty by giving better service than the customers expected.

"Girls!" he would begin, "when you promise to deliver a product in three weeks, get it to them in a fortnight! Do more," he would say, "not less."

In the same way, a large door promises to reveal a large area but disappoints when the area is small. It is far better to exceed expectations. A door size should match the spirit of a place.

If a door is too large and the space is small, reduce the scale of the furnishings to give the room a feeling of spaciousness. Hang a painting with a scene or landscape that will seem to enlarge the room.

If you have a small door or passageway that opens into a large area . . .

The spirit of a room is expressed by its entrance. Important rooms, such as gathering rooms, should have important entrances. In a gathering room a small door broadcasts, "Don't come in." Openings leading to gathering rooms should be wide enough to accommodate more than one person.

Add some flourishes to a small entrance. Position an important statue, flood the thresholds with bright lights, or place an area carpet next to the threshold. Dressing up the entrance will match it to the large space entered.

If your door does not open flat against the adjoining wall . . .

The Chinese believe that evil spirits lurk in hidden areas behind doors. A door that opens only partially signals caution in an unconscious way, and we must give credence to what we feel in the pit of our stomach.

If it is not possible to reverse the swing of the door, hang a mirror to reflect the empty space behind the door.

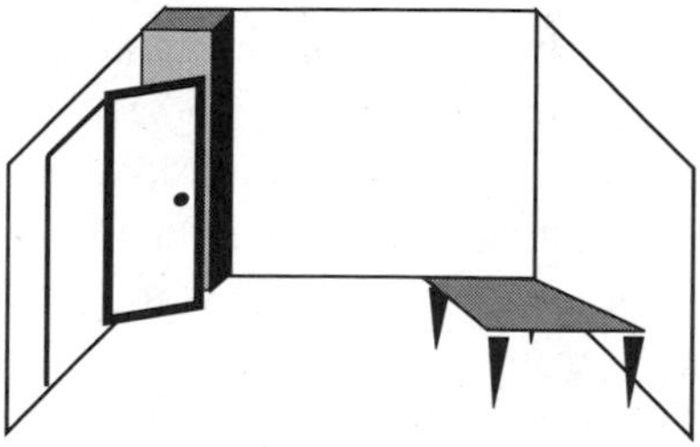

A door that does not open flat against the wall is inauspicious.

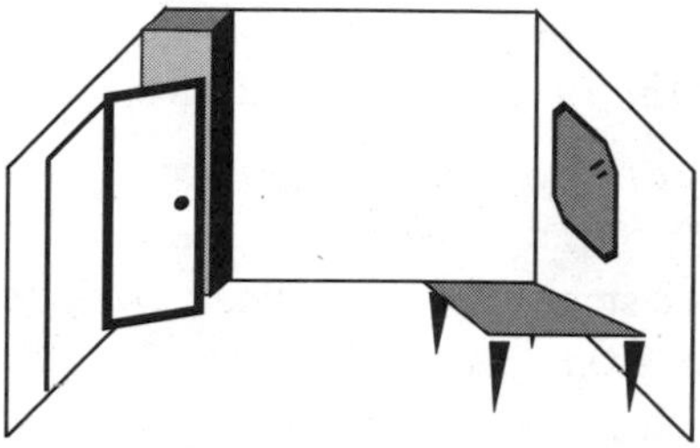

A mirror reflecting the empty space behind the wall cures this condition.

If you have glass inserts in doors or glass doors . . .

While it is beneficial to be able to see who might be at the door, it is not a good idea to be seen before you are aware of visitors. We need to feel shielded from visual intrusion. Few want to live in a fishbowl.

Why doors are designed with clearglass inserts is anyone's guess. Most of the time they are curtained or have opaqued glass.

If changing the door is not an option, screen the interior activity area from view with a plant, a dividing screen, or any appropriate piece of furniture.

If your home has an entrance door larger in proportion to the facade of a house than a mouth is to a face . . .

A door is an opening that protects the vital ingredients in a home. When it's too big, we are exposed and vulnerable.

If the front door is larger in proportion than a mouth is to a face, mount a light over its center to visually reduce the apparent size; the picture your eye records is reduced in sharpness at the perimeter of an image because it is in shadow. Another possibility is to paint the door a soft, dark color from the rest of the home to help it fade rather than stand out from the rest of the facade.

If the front door appears smaller in proportion to the facade of a home than a mouth is to a face . . .

A home with a tiny front door minimizes access and makes us feel unwelcome and constrained to enter.

Add importance to a small door. Station large objects like plants or sculptures on either side, paint the area around the door the same color as the door to make it seem bigger, or mount lights on three sides to add visual importance.

If you cannot see the majority of a room upon entering . . .

We feel more secure when we are able to stake out a territory. It is common to feel safer and more in control when the parameters of a space are in view.

In many cases repositioning one piece of furniture can open up a view of a room. However, when there is an architectural reason for the obstruction, position a mirror to view the unviewable part.

18

STAIRS

Stairs, like life, have their ups and downs. Ascending or descending can be a metaphor for how we travel through our existence. Stairs lead us to other areas of a home, and if they are uncomfortable or precarious we may not choose to go where they lead.

A staircase must be secure, inviting, and easy to locate and negotiate. While providing a separation for the different areas, it must be a link in the network of home. Because traversing a staircase is harder than moving through other passages, other mitigating factors must be built into the experience.

Next time you walk up a staircase, notice if you are engaged in a physical struggle or pleasantly distracted by the scene around you.

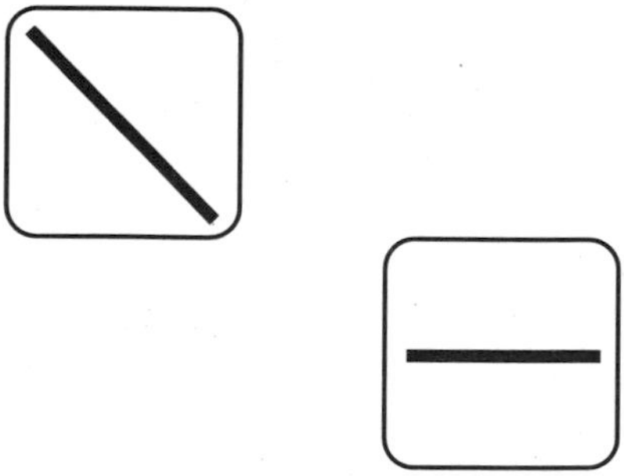

The diagonal line of a stairway demands more attention than do horizontal lines like the tops of most furniture.

Stairs are vertical hallways, and their dynamic diagonal line lures us to mount. The location of a stairwell is important in this regard, since you don't want a staircase to lead away from the heart of the home. A staircase directly in line with an entrance door can, in some cases, gnaw away at family unity; so can a descending and an ascending staircase off the entrance (see Chapter 13).

TEST

SCORE 2 for stairs with high risers.

SCORE 1 for stairs with open risers.

SCORE 2 for a home with a main spiral staircase.

SCORE 2 for a home with more than three separate staircases having more than four steps each.

The total negative score could be 7. Naturally, curing all negative conditions is the ideal to strive toward. If you have scored almost one half of the total score, consider it a warning signal and attend to making some changes as soon as possible. Being surrounded by the best conditions helps you thrive!

If your home has stairs with higher-than-normal risers . . .

Any ascent or descent is experienced as difficult when its slope is too steep to be negotiated comfortably. You might think twice before running upstairs to fetch something when the climb seems too arduous. Life in a home with stairs with higher-than-normal risers may seen generally more difficult.

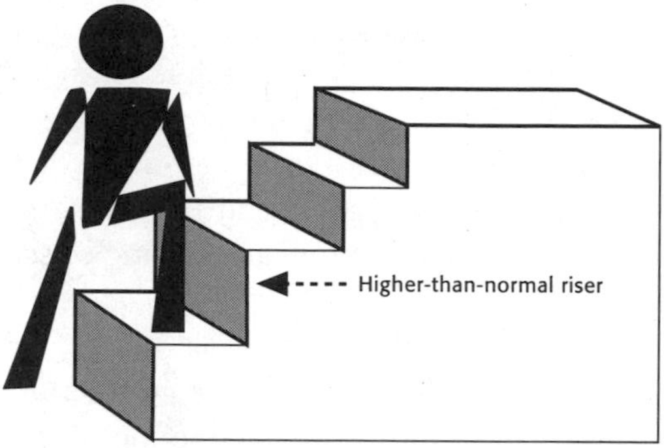

Only structural changes can alter the actual climb, but you can keep in-demand items like scissors, bandages, and towels on all floors to alleviate running up and down the stairs quite so often. Positioning a wind-sensitive object, a boldly painted wall covering, or a large painting or poster at the extremes of a staircase can invigorate our chi for the climb. Filling a wall next to the staircase with ornaments or pictures can provide a reward for the effort of making the climb.

If your stairs have open risers . . .

Ascending a staircase with no backing to stop a foot from careening through the opening is at best slightly unnerv-

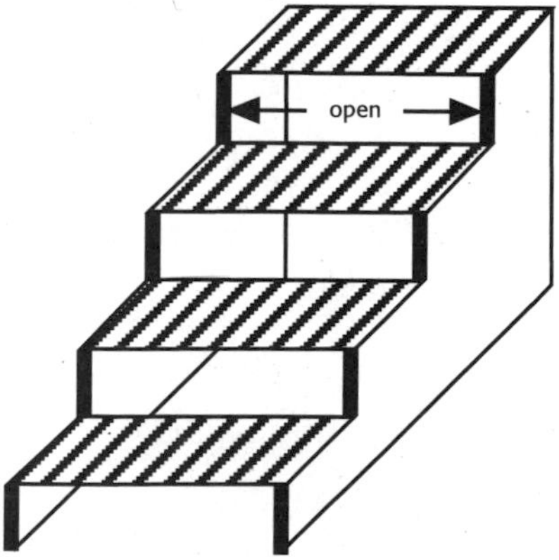

Floating treads or stairs without risers are inauspicious.

ing and at worst treacherous. Again, a staircase provides a transition from one part of the home to another and must be secure, inviting, and easy to negotiate.

Hang solid objects, like a basket of ivy or decorative globes, behind the opening in the treads to arrest the eye as well as provide a greater feeling of security.

If you have a spiral staircase . . .

A spiral staircase is harder to negotiate than a regular staircase. Moreover, the corkscrew motion of traversing a spiral can make us feel slightly off balance and hence insecure.

Connect the different floors through color, texture, or similar aesthetic choice. This will lessen any feeling of disorientation caused by the circular motion of the climb. For example, the railing might be painted in the color theme of the downstairs room, and the carpeting on the treads might be the same as the upstairs floor covering.

Be sure handrails are secure and steady. If they are too thin or insubstantial, pad them to thicken.

If your home has more than three staircases . . .

Originally homes were built with more than one staircase to separate the family members' paths from those of the servants.

Multistaircase homes are called *split-levels*, which certainly conveys the feeling this sort of floor plan evokes! It is not surprising that divorce and parent-child divisiveness are exacerbated in a dwelling that splits the space into many parts and separates the people from one another.

To reverse the schism in family life, a central theme should be established. Create a strong collective thread with color, pattern, or a collection of similar objects repeated throughout the entire home.

Any collections, from shells to antique pillboxes, can serve as a uniting entity for an entire house. If you are not a collector, use family photographs and place them in freestanding frames on shelves, cabinets, and tables. This will not only unite the experience of a home but also strengthen the feeling of family.

19

Ceilings

The word *ceiling* means to overlay or obscure the original. According to this definition ceilings veil reality.

We should duplicate as best we can the feeling of expansiveness evoked when looking up. Unobstructed views above us help us feel unencumbered. Therefore, any element that blocks out or inhibits this feeling, like low beams, bypasses our accustomed experience.

We need to pay attention to the position of exposed beams. On an unconscious level we know beams are a structure's skeleton—the bones of a framework that supports the final form. If a bone is broken, we are impaired. If a beam crumbles, a home collapses. Seating and sleeping areas are best located without beams directly overhead, especially in areas with earthquake potential.

Test

Score 1 for any ceiling that is three and a half times a person's height in a space that is used for sitting or reclining.

Score 2 for any ceiling that can be touched when standing upright.

Score 1 for each slanted ceiling reaching lower than six and a half feet.

SCORE 2 if beams cover more than a third of the total ceiling space and can be touched when standing.

SCORE 2 if a beam is over a seating or sleeping area.

The total negative score could be 8. Naturally, curing all negative conditions is the ideal to strive toward. If you have scored almost one half of the total score, consider it a warning signal and attend to making some changes as soon as possible. Being surrounded by the best conditions helps you thrive!

If a ceiling over a sitting or reclining area is three and a half times a person's height . . .

Height often equals might. We are intimidated by those much larger than we are. As a child I stood on a chair when I had something important to tell my parents. Being equal in height gave me a feeling of being equal in power. I believed I was better able to get my message across when I appeared taller.

Churches, state houses, and other important buildings often have rooms whose ceilings reach the stratosphere. They are designed to promote a sense of awe and wonder. Created to diminish an individual's importance, these spaces flaunt their superiority over the individuals. Fine for an institution but unsuitable as a family nest.

My husband and I enjoy dining al fresco on an enclosed deck off our gathering room. It is a rather small space, measuring only six by eight feet, but it has an eighteen-foot-high ceiling. When sitting at the table we felt as if we were seated in a cylinder. The ceiling was too high to provide a sense of intimacy. My cure for this inauspicious feng shui was to hang an upside-down umbrella from the ceiling. Now we feel as if we are nestled under a canopy of intimacy in our tropical paradise.

Any cure that would lower the ceiling or give visual weight to the bottom half of the room would work. Install a ceiling fan, hang pictures at eye level when seated, or paint the lower half of the room a lighter color.

If your ceilings are too low . . .

Upon his return from a trip to Egypt, a six-foot plus friend regaled me with stories about being bonked in the head when touring the pyramids. Even if your head doesn't collide with the ceiling of a room, a low ceiling can make you feel trapped and claustrophobic.

Lighten and brighten to create a spacious feeling in a room with a low ceiling. Focus attention on light from electrical fixtures or windows. Anything that helps the eye rest on an object closer to the floor will make the ceiling seem higher. Place a cut crystal bowl, a shiny metal planter, or an eye-catching art object on a low table or floor. Mirrors or polished metal surfaces positioned to reflect a person entering a room can direct attention away from a low ceiling and make it seem less oppressive.

If you have a choice, a room with a low ceiling should be used for sitting rather than standing activities.

If your home has slanted ceilings that are lower on one end than standing height . . .

When it is deliberate, we can enjoy low spaces. I once cured a slanted ceiling over a desk by tenting the ceiling to change the atmosphere from oppressive to festive. The space underneath felt secure, much like the feeling we had as children when crawling underneath tables to create cozy play spaces.

Tenting a slanted ceiling can make it feel festive and secure.

However, when a seating unit is not a viable selection underneath the lower end of a slanted ceiling, place a cabinet or table against the low wall so you are forced to stand at a distance from the lowest area.

If you face toward the lower end but are not underneath it, mount a mirror on the lowest part of the ceiling to make it visually disappear.

If you have too many or inappropriately placed ceiling beams . . .

Imagine walking along a river nestled in a canyon. The day is glorious and cloudless, and fragrances of wildflowers permeate the air. While following the flight of a songbird, you notice a boulder above you perched at the edge of a canyon wall. Suddenly you freeze, fearing the rock above could come careening down. The tranquil feeling is lost.

Although not as dramatic, beams overhead instill an unconscious sense of danger in homes built in geologically unstable areas. Because China is a land with earthquakes, beams are considered ominous.

For those of us in areas not subjected to earthquakes, it is more important to consider the amount of beams and their distance from the floor. When beams repeat themselves frequently like bars on a prison door, they feel negative. If they are positioned over a seating area, we may feel threatened in the same way as walking under a boulder perched on a canyon wall. Living optimally requires freedom from fear, real or implied by an environment.

Position seating or sleeping areas out from under a beam. If that's impossible, mirror the underside of the beam or hang a wind-sensitive object from the beam to flutter and break up the feeling of oppression. Strong light highlighting a seating area is another way to reduce the implied burden of an overhead beam. Since light commands attention, you may not notice the beam and won't be affected by its presence.

20

WINDOWS

Windows are our eyes to the world. We see and are seen through them. In the same way as our inner being is revealed by an expression in our eyes, windows communicate volumes about a home's occupants.

Passing a home either without windows or with all the shades drawn produces a nagging uneasiness. What are they hiding? We feel vulnerable knowing we can't be seen and would not be helped if a need arose.

Social theorist Jane Jacobs suggested that places lacking "eyes on the street" will ultimately be unsafe places to live. It was the grandmas perched in chairs by windows that helped keep city neighborhoods safe. When brownstones were replaced by high-rise apartments, the streets lost their "grandma patrol." Now positioned high above street level, these sentries lost their effectiveness by virtue of visual and vocal distance.

When we're inside, windows provide a connection to the world. I feel less isolated when facing a window while working in my home office. As I pound my computer's keyboard, the occasional passing car, person, or animal counters my feeling of being sequestered from life.

Windows frame a portrait of nature or human-made panoramas. A window can afford a home's occupant a dazzling scene, either of a natural landscape or one that is shaped by inspiration. Gardens can nurture us on a deep level, while a cityscape's energy can motivate. Windows are the kaleidoscopic lens through which we view these marvels.

The appropriate direction of a window's view depends on a room's function. A western window next to a teenager's desk will impede studying. The glare of a setting sun can frustrate the concentration of even the most diligent student.

TEST

SCORE 1 if a room feels as if there are too many windows.

SCORE 3 for any room without windows.

SCORE 1 for each room that has more than three windows per door.

SCORE 2 for any room with a window across from its entrance door.

SCORE 2 for any window that does not open.

SCORE 2 for each room in which most of the windows face the severest weather.

SCORE 2 if a home does not have any windows facing the rising sun.

SCORE 1 for any work room with its seating area facing a western exposure.

SCORE 1 for windows above street level that are lower than knee height.

Score 1 for each window positioned over a toilet.

Score 1 if you do not have a window in a bathroom.

Score 1 if a dining room has mostly windowed wall.

Score 2 if there are no windows in the front of the house.

The total negative score could be 20. Naturally, curing all negative conditions is the ideal to strive toward. If you have scored almost one half of the total score, consider it a warning signal and attend to making some changes as soon as possible. Being surrounded by the best conditions helps you thrive!

If a room has too many windows . . .

A home is to a human as a cocoon is to a butterfly. It provides a safe nurturing space in which to mature. When Philip Johnson built his all-glass house in Connecticut in 1959, he hoped to start a contemporary trend. However, his concept did not mesh with human needs. A sheltered feeling can protect us from more than just elements. Occupants inside an all-glass home feel exposed in a way that is not conducive to the feeling of home as sanctuary.

Make sure there is at least one area in a room that feels shielded from the outside. Window coverings, of course, are an alternative, although not necessarily the best one. While they protect, they may also block both a view and natural light. Strategically positioned plants, sculptures, or any other aesthetically acceptable object between a window and a room's interior can instill a feeling of security.

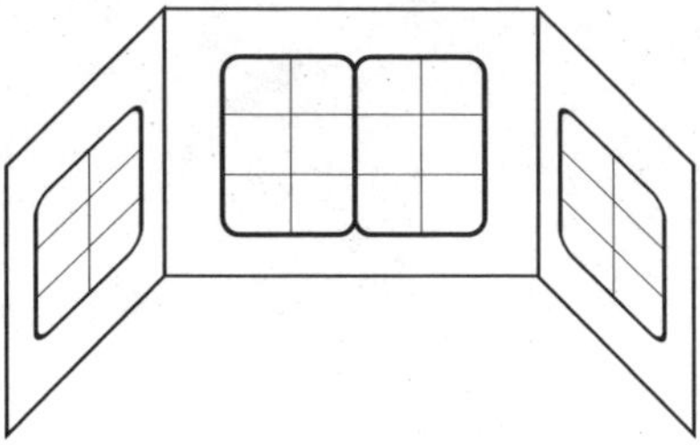

Inauspicious

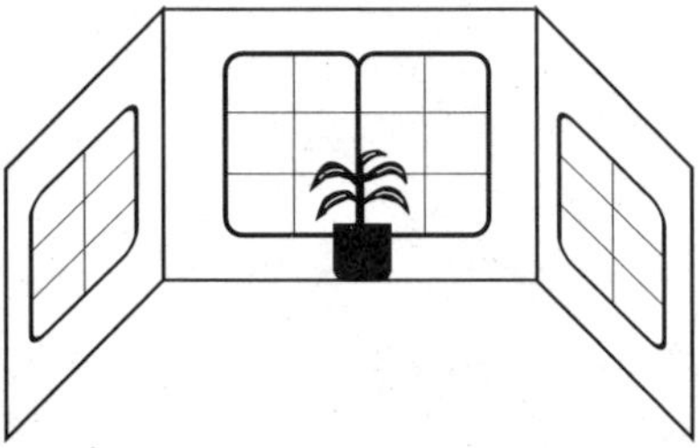

Cure

Recently I advised a family whose main gathering room consisted of three walls of windows to hang a twelve-inch vertical strip of mirror across from the entrance door. Seeing one's image upon entering helps reinforce a sense of place inside a room.

If a room has no windows . . .

Lack of windows deprives us of sensory stimulation that is essential to our well-being. Workers in windowless environments experience the stress of being out of sync with the cadence of daylight. Most workplaces are illuminated uniformly regardless of season or time of day, despite the fact that unvarying artificial light is not harmonious with the ebb and flow of our internal rhythms. Our intrinsic biological needs are eclipsed by other considerations when we are separated from the outside by a lack of windows.

If a structure cannot be changed to incorporate windows, compensate by providing an overpowering alternative experience. Prisoners often become singularly involved in activities such as pumping iron or reading the law to counteract the deprivation of connection.

In a home, install a grow light over a plant, hang a large photo or picture of an outdoor scene, or have a bowl with recirculating water in any area without windows. You may want to intensify the relief these provide by hanging a mirror across from these cures.

If you have a room with more than three windows per door . . .

Ancient feng shui warns that children will be disobedient when occupying a room with more than three windows per door.

When I first read this rule, I scratched my head and wondered why in the world that would be true. Then I remembered my elementary school days, when I was reprimanded by my teacher for whispering to my friends. Suddenly I'd be absorbed in observing something outside the classroom's window. A fluttering leaf, a squirrel scampering across the playground, or the letters on a license plate of a parked car would capture my wavering attention. The teacher's admonishments would fall on deaf ears.

Ah, I thought, this feng shui rule is telling us that in some cases too many windows can be distracting.

We love our windows! They are less expensive and more energy-efficient to make than they were in ancient China, so having fewer windows is not the solution for our contemporary needs and aesthetics.

To extract the essence from this ancient rule, we need only remember that a scene outside a window can sometimes be an undesirable distraction. So, to eliminate the possibility of having disobedient children, simply remember to position them away from a window when instructing them in prescribed behavior. Feng shui is, after all, the art of placement. Position the child differently, not the window.

If there is a window directly across from the entrance door of a room . . .

In most cases it is better to have our attention remain fixed within a space we are entering. A window across from a door may distract us from focusing within the room. The central activity area—the desk, the seating units in an office, or the bed in a bedroom—should engage our visual attention before it is diverted elsewhere.

A rippling transparent curtain in front of an open window will encourage us to remain visually inside, as will any imposing object placed in the floor space between the window and the entrance. The more senses this object engages, the better it will serve this purpose. A fish tank or a bubbling indoor fountain engages our sight and hearing, and a diffuser with an appropriate scent engages the visual and olfactory senses.

If your home has windows that won't open . . .

The term *sick buildings* has become synonymous with structures having windows that won't open. Without a source of fresh air, bacteria, mildew, and secondhand smoke are circulated and shared by all.

In addition to the obvious health hazards, negative emotional states are aroused by the absence of fresh air. We feel mentally trapped and tired when we are separated from the Tao of life. A brain needs oxygen to fuel its optimal performance, and sharpness or mental edge deteriorates when we are forced to breathe stale air.

"A breath of fresh air" is an expression we use to describe someone who brings to a situation a refreshing uniqueness. Make sure a personal environment evokes the same reaction.

If fresh air cannot penetrate a structure, try these alternatives:

- Install an indoor fountain whose aerating waters can produce negative ions to charge a lifeless atmosphere. Place this fountain close to the most frequently used areas.
- Place a tiny fan underneath the leaves of a desktop plant to simulate leaves fluttering in the breeze.
- If opportunities don't exist to make physical changes, try an audiocassette of a babbling brook, birds singing, or other natural sounds.

Be inventive. Replicating a natural sight, sound, smell, or motion will surely lift your spirit.

If you have too many windows facing the direction of the severest weather . . .

Windows in the direction of the severest weather expose the interior of our homes to extremes. In the northeastern United States, a window to the north exposes us to the chill of a winter day, while in the southern states a western exposure can magnify the heat at the end of a summer day. Since we need to use energy to deflect any inauspicious condition, we dissipate personal power when we are located near windows that radiate the discomfort of extreme weather.

Move all seating or working areas away from windows subjected to the severest weather or buffer seating areas with window coverings. Install curtains with insulated lining or hang a tapestry or heavy fabric on the problem wall to shield the cold or heat.

If your home has no windows facing the rising sun . . .

Having a home filled with light in the morning assures us of getting off to a good start each day. Sunlight begets optimism. Simplistic as it may seem, we feel infused with optimism when facing the rising sun.

A home without sufficient windows facing the rising sun should be filled with artificial light and elements associated with sunlight. Make sure the light is not monotonous. Outside, the light is dappled because it shines through either vegetation or buildings or is stippled by its passage behind clouds. Unrelenting light is an extreme that can be experienced as negative over the long haul. We recoil from fluorescent overhead lighting in part because of its insistent uniform distribution. Individual lamps positioned throughout a space can counteract the stress of uniform ceiling lighting.

If you have too many windows facing the setting sun in rooms where afternoon activities requiring concentration take place . . .

When I was ill as a child, our family physician instructed my mother to record my temperature at 4:00 P.M. to determine if I was on the mend. Even if my fever was normal during the rest of the day, it would elevate during the late afternoon if I was not completely restored to health.

The sinking afternoon sun puts a strain on our psyche. While the sun slides down toward the horizon, we need to revitalize our energies for the remaining waking hours.

Do not face the setting sun when engaged in an activity that requires concentration. If there is no alternative to moving your activity from a western window, try repositioning it slightly to avoid a direct glare in your eyes. A plant, a screen, a framed stained-glass piece, or any perforated item can be an effective shield between the sun's glare and your eyes.

If there are windows on upper floors installed lower than knee height . . .

Windows installed close to the floor can make you feel uncomfortable. Standing next to a window that has a bottom ledge below knee level can produce a feeling of insecurity, especially if the window is on an upper floor.

Sliding glass windows or glass doors opening to a deck or terrace are exempt because they open out to a platform that would clearly block a fall. Without benefit of a terrace, a solid wall at knee height promotes a sense of security.

Place a solid, grounded object in front of a low window. It will distance the person both physically and emotionally from the low window. Plants are ideal because, while they provide visual security, they are positioned in a perfect place to thrive. A hassock, low table, or small chair can also provide the necessary relief.

If you have a large bathroom window positioned behind or in front of a toilet . . .

Unless privacy is secured by vegetation or distance, when you can see out, others can see in. We need to feel completely at ease in spaces devoted to private necessities.

My sister used to live in New York City in a pre-World War II building. Positioned directly behind her toilet was a giant window. To cure this negative feng shui, we changed the transparent glass to opaque. Other options would include hanging a framed piece of stained glass in front of the window, curtaining it, or screening it with plants or other decorative objects.

If you have no bathroom windows . . .

Although a view outside is not absolutely essential in a bathroom, circulating fresh air is.

If there is no window or air draft designed to clear and replenish the air quality, place a plant with a pronounced pleasant fragrance inside this room. This revives the air quality and provides a natural deodorizer.

If the size of the room permits, install a small recirculating fountain and keep a few drops of natural aromas in the water to deodorize the air. Or keep a candle and a pack of matches on the back of the commode. The occupant can use this option to dissipate any discomfort caused by not being able to naturally adjust the air quality.

If there are too many windows in a dining room . . .

When I first read about the ancient Chinese feng shui dictate that cautioned against having many windows in a dining room, I wondered why that room and not others. Then I realized that windows are supposed to provide a pleasant view, one that demands some attention. Hopefully they frame the outside world in its finest form.

A dining room provides more than a table on which to consume nutrients. It is a gathering spot to ingest emotional and spiritual nourishment. Whether we eat when alone or dine with others, too many windows in a dining area can be a distraction from receiving this benefit.

Position the diners so they don't face the windows, or hang a curtain that will permit light to filter in without allowing a clear view of the outdoors. Sometimes a

Position those you want to pay attention to you so they are not facing windows.

folding room divider can screen out distracting views and can be relocated when not in use.

If there are no windows at the front of a home . . .

Since I live in Florida, I tend to wear sunglasses while out and about. Often, when entering a building, I forget to take them off. When I am with my husband, however, he is quick to remind me. He believes eyes are the key to effective communication and should not be concealed.

A home's facade is like a face, and the windows are like the eyes. Without windows a house looks concealed, lonely, detached, and unfriendly. A building without front windows says, "I don't want to see you, and I don't want you to see me."

Short of installing new windows, place objects that communicate your uniqueness to the neighborhood. A

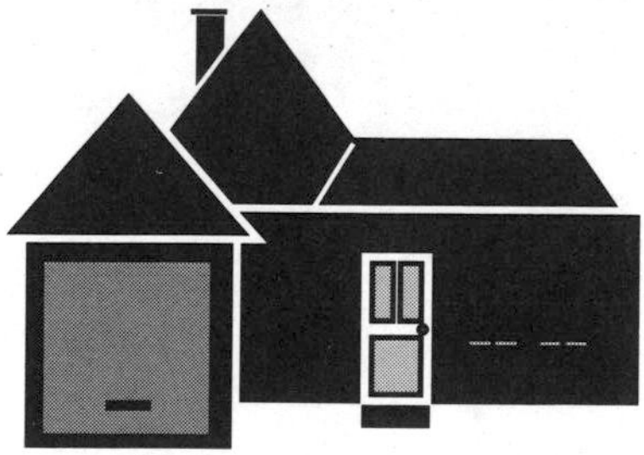

A house with no front windows is unfriendly.

home with a hummingbird feeder, a wind sock, a birdbath on the lawn, and suet feeders hung from trees expresses something about the occupants. A mailbox shaped like a book could indicate the home of a writer or an avid reader. Let your proclivities hang out a little if your home doesn't have windows in its facade.

The Cures

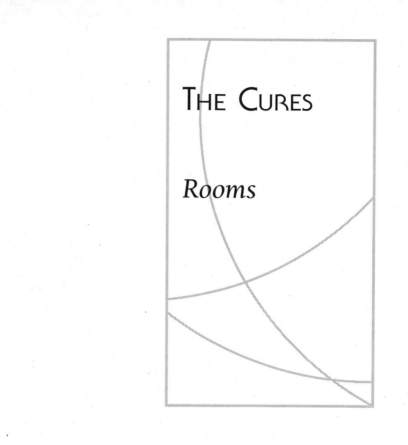

Rooms

21

Gathering Rooms

The gathering room serves as a home's epicenter. Whether it's for informal conversation, watching TV, playing games, reading, or merely being, a gathering space improves or inhibits optimum functioning.

Although you might have several rooms that serve as common meeting rooms, each should be distinguished by facilitating different activities. We may converse in one gathering room, watch TV in another, and play Ping-Pong in a third. It is imperative to define a room's main use before arranging furniture, lighting, or accessories. Dual-purpose rooms usually have the same fate as reversible jackets. One side dominates, and the other gets worn infrequently. At best it's hard to serve two masters.

I grew up in a home with a "living room" that was off-limits to my sister and me. We would pass through it quickly, hoping not to spill our sodas on my mother's *good* carpet. We felt like interlopers on a theater's stage. We passed through that room to reach our family's "den," a converted porch eight feet wide and eighteen feet long. The sofas in the den were, by necessity, arranged against one wall. There we all sat like ducks in a row. No wonder we didn't talk to each other in that room.

Being able to view a TV forces us to arrange sofas to face a screen instead of other seating groups. Closed seating, where seats face each other, is designed to facilitate conversation. How a family functions together depends in part on how the interior spaces are designed. A family that expects a seating arrangement for watching TV to be equally good for conversation will be sadly disappointed. Family members have to decide which activity is more important and arrange their spaces accordingly.

How often have you sat down in someone's main space and found yourself in competition with a TV? Recently I was visiting a home where the TV was kept on the entire time I was there even though no one was watching it. It is hard to be engaged in razor-sharp conversation when canned laughter floats through the air.

If you hope to have a family that loves spending time together engaged in productive interactions, design a space where activities that promote togetherness can flourish. To gather is to call together, and the room must encourage interaction.

TEST

SCORE 2 if there is no path leading into a gathering space from the main door.

SCORE 2 if the arrangement does not support the room's main activity.

SCORE 1 if the gathering space is not visually connected to the outside either by windows or by a long view through another room's windows.

SCORE 1 if access to other parts of the home is hidden from sight or sound.

Score 2 if TV is the central focus of the most frequently used gathering room.

Score 2 if the main seating faces away from the main entrance.

The total negative score could be 10. Naturally, curing all negative conditions is the ideal to strive toward. If you have scored almost one half of the total score, consider it a warning signal and attend to making some changes as soon as possible. Being surrounded by the best conditions helps you thrive!

If there is no pathway from an entrance door into a gathering space . . .

I was asked by a builder of a large development to evaluate his architect's plans before he began to build. He wanted to be assured that his homes were aligned with the best feng shui principles. After studying the blueprints, I determined that the worst flaw was the lack of a well-lit definite pathway leading from the entrance foyer to the main gathering space.

The entrance was a long narrow space blocked off from a view of other rooms by a wall at the end. At the

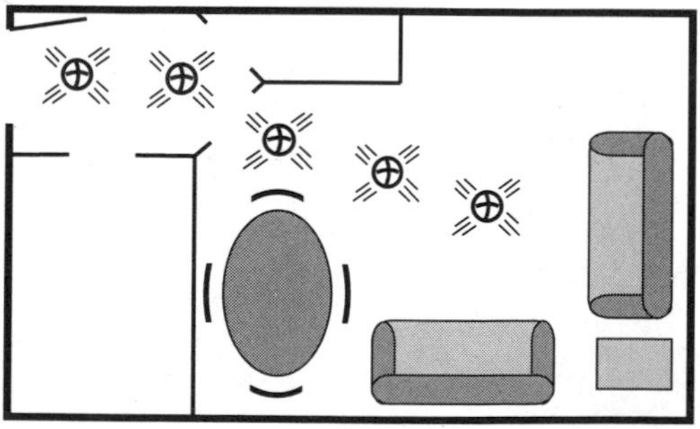

Create a path into a gathering room using a series of lights.

end of the hallway you had to turn to enter the next room, the dining room. Only after you turned another ninety degrees did you see the main gathering room in the distance. By that time you felt as if you were driving down an unfamiliar street searching for house numbers.

The cure was rather simple. By adjusting the shape of the wall at the end of the hallway and installing three lights to illuminate a passageway into the gathering space, we created a larger, easy-to-see, well-lit path that led you into the heart of this home.

A row of lights helps define the pathway to a gathering room, but there are many other possibilities as well—color, wall embellishments, flooring, and plants can also be used to lead the eye. Where the eye leads, the body will follow.

If you have a modest-sized entrance, you need to install beacons that invite inspection. Placement of fur-

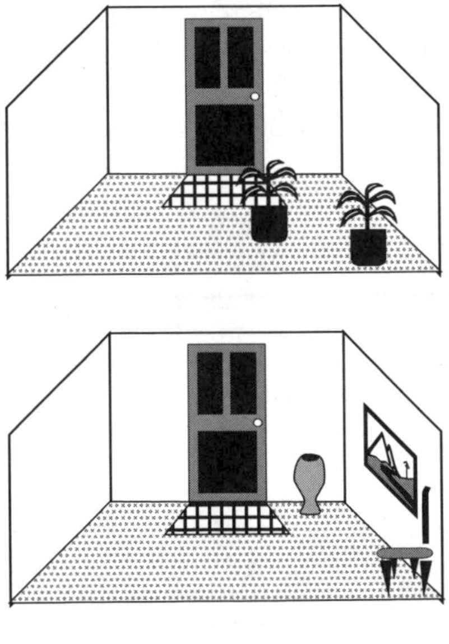

Cures to create a visual pathway to the center of a space

niture, color, and repetitive elements leading toward the center of a home can create a visual pathway to the center of a space. Consider how the flooring, lighting, height of wall decoration, and color of walls enhance the visual path into a home's heart.

If the room is not arranged to support the intended main activity . . .

A room set up for two dissimilar activities makes engaging in one of them difficult.

In most cases a room will have one main use. If a secondary use area (like a work space in a bedroom or a home accounting corner in a dining room) is either the first sight seen when entering that room or is in direct view from the room's main seating area, the positive intention of the room may be undermined. Who wants to be reminded of bills due while they are dining? What nightmares could result from having our desks be the last thing we see before falling asleep? Do not place secondary activities in dominant positions. Obscure them from sight from the entrance or main seating area.

If your gathering space is not visually connected to the outside . . .

Just as our experiences reach beyond the borders of a home, events in the world come inside to change our lives. When we don't have free egress to the outdoors, we feel stir-crazy. Whether it's physical or visual, no one likes being denied access to options.

Positioning a mirror to reflect a view from a distant window can be one way to cure this condition. When there is no access to a view, stage a scene via pictures, artifacts, vegetation, or fountains to suggest the outer world, real or imagined.

If your gathering room is not in a central position . . .

A gathering room is the hub of the various rooms in a home and thus should be connected in some way to all of them. All family members need emotional tune-ups to keep a connection to family life prime. Our lives outside of the family sometimes sap our stamina, and returning to a nest that replenishes each individual is imperative to a family's health. A central gathering room can be like the eye in a hurricane, the calm inside a swirling vortex.

A swirling fan, a radio softly playing music, or a gurgling fountain can be the stimulant to attract members to this room if it is not central. A wind-sensitive object that produces a pleasant sound near an open window or forced-air heating vent can beckon family members to gather.

If TV is the main focus in a gathering room . . .

I am flabbergasted to discover how many homes have in their center a TV in lieu of a place to serve as a forum for exchanging ideas or engaging in activities together. If there is no alternative place for the TV, position an ottoman or chair with rollers in front of the TV to complete a conversational arrangement. Move it aside when appropriate. Put the TV in a cabinet, throw a decorative cloth over it, or devise something unique—just cover the TV's screen. Out-of-sight helps keep things out of mind.

If the main seating group faces away from the room's main entrance . . .

The instinct to keep our backs to the wall facing an entrance goes back to the cave-dwelling days, when this position gave people a chance to react quickly to a sur-

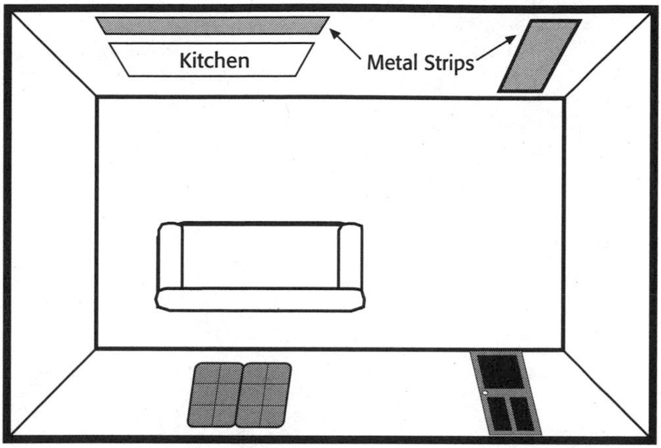

Use reflective surfaces, such as metal strips or mirrors, to provide a view of the room's main entrance.

prise visit by a predator and in many cases meant the difference between life and death. Although it is not as integral to our survival today, it is part of our species' memory, and we feel more relaxed when we are positioned to see those entering a room.

Neighbors of mine placed their gathering room's sofa away from the entrance because the view out the back through their kitchen is spectacular. Still, they felt slightly uncomfortable facing away from the home's front window and door and asked me for suggestions.

A mirror positioned to reflect the front door and window would be an easy solution. However, since they didn't like mirrors, I suggested thick slices of polished metal that would appear to be an architectural detail and still be a reflective surface. We positioned one strip at the edge of a wall to reflect the front door and one strip over the kitchen's pass-through to look like a decorative trim.

22

Dining Rooms

Standing over a bowl of chips and salsa at a counter, wolfing down a sandwich purchased at a fast-food emporium, or snacking in an automobile, Americans often do not use mealtimes as meeting times. However, eliminating dining as a pleasurable experience can be detrimental to an optimum existence.

When I was growing up, families usually ate together. The moms sat family members down to a "good" breakfast before everyone scattered for the day's activities. Children walked home to lunch, and dinner was eaten when the fathers returned home from work.

When I became a mother, things were different. Both parents worked, and commuting timetables dictated that many breakfasts and dinners took second place to business needs. Lunch was eaten at school, and dinner times varied.

Feng shui's ideas support unity within family life, and dining is a central activity. In the best of all possible worlds we should dine together with loved ones in a contained space that is accessible to the food preparation area but not in its midst. The focus of the room is the table, and other artifacts should not take away from this focus.

TEST

SCORE 1 for each chair around a dining table that is not backed by a wall.

SCORE 1 if there is a pathway behind a row of dining room seats.

SCORE 2 if you can see out too many windows or see other rooms while seated at the dining room table.

SCORE 1 if a mirror in a dining area reflects another room, the outdoors, or the diners.

SCORE 1 if there are more than two extra chairs for the number of people who typically eat together.

SCORE 2 if your dining table is too large for easy communication with other diners.

SCORE 2 if you dine in a room that is more cluttered than stark.

SCORE 1 if there is no lighting over the table.

The total negative score could be 11. Naturally, curing all negative conditions is the ideal to strive toward. If you have scored almost one half of the total score, consider it a warning signal and attend to making some changes as soon as possible. Being surrounded by the best conditions helps you thrive!

If your dining table is not surrounded by walls . . .

My cat almost jumps out of her skin when taken by surprise during her mealtimes. Our basic instincts tell us

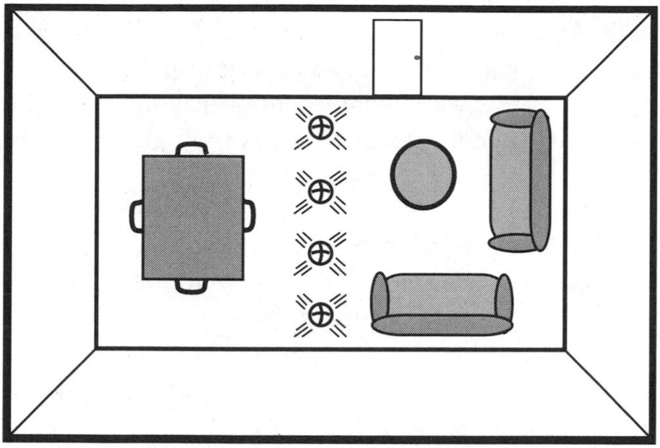

Use lighting to create a wall and divide living and dining areas.

to protect our feast from predators. Even without predators, our senses are heightened while we eat. Having no walls behind us does nothing to reduce a gnawing alertness.

If dining and living areas are contiguous, install a screen, plant, sculpture, bookcase, or wind-sensitive object as a substitute for a solid wall. Ceiling spots throwing pools of light toward the floor can substitute for a solid wall. Installing colored lightbulbs in the row of spotlights will add a festive air to the dividing line between a dining area and another space.

If you have a pathway behind a row of seats . . .

You can provide a warning signal for persons sitting with their backs to a pathway by altering the flooring in the pathway or installing a movement-sensitive object that will vibrate, chime, or rustle when walked by.

Carpeted pathways are normally soundless, while an uncarpeted floor when walked upon with shoes will create enough of a sound to alert those with their backs to the pathway. If changing or adding flooring is not an option, a movement-sensitive object that will rustle when walked by might be the solution. I have suggested buying a small hand-painted canvas rug to place over carpeting because when stepped upon it will produce a sound that is both distinctive and loud enough to be heard.

Even if there is only one wall of windows in a dining room, be sure to seat those with the shortest attention span with their backs to these windows. Teenagers are prime candidates for these spots.

To shield diners from a distracting view of other rooms, try the cures given for contiguous living and dining areas.

If you have a dining room with views that distract diners . . .

Like a hand fluttering to signal good-bye, movement attracts attention, as do bright light, intense color, and dynamic shapes. More often than not the scene outside is filled with nature's agitation, a plethora of colors and shapes as well as the sharpness of daylight or the electric glimmer of evening's lights. How can you be surrounded by windows and not be distracted?

Mealtimes are a forum for the digestion of conversation and food. Keep distractions at a minimum. Redirect attention away from the windows. An engaging centerpiece can be a magnet for focus, as can electric light or candles in the center of the table. By covering windows with a sheer fabric treatment, you can camouflage outside distractions while allowing light to penetrate.

If you have mirrors hanging in a dining room that reflect another room, the outdoors, or diners at the table . . .

Seeing the outdoors or other rooms through a mirror is just as distracting as viewing them directly. Try the cures listed for the preceding two problems or simply move the mirrors.

When mirrors reflect the diners, replace the mirrors with other decorative objects. Like many teenagers, I was self-conscious. When we had company for dinner, I was overly concerned with my appearance. I would constantly sneak peaks at myself by looking into the gleaming surface of the dinner knife to check my image. Although sometimes we cannot remove all distractions like knives, reflective surfaces that grab our attention should be kept to a minimum in a dining room.

If there are more than two extra chairs for the number of people who typically eat together . . .

Keep extra chairs for occasional visitors nearby, but do not have more than two extra chairs at a table. Empty chairs at a dining room table, like empty bedrooms, can remind us of who might be missing. When a space is appropriate, it will feel as comfortable as properly fitting clothes—neither too tight nor too loose.

If a table is too big and another-sized table is unavailable, try using the other end of the table for a display area. Arrange photos, artifacts, or other decorative accessories to change the appearance from an empty table to an exciting presentation platform.

If you dine at a table whose shape precludes communicating with others seated there . . .

My rule of thumb for dinner parties is not to invite more people than I can comfortably talk to at the table. With few exceptions, like sprawling Thanksgiving holidays, I find it pointless to entertain people with whom I cannot personally communicate.

Long rectangles are fine for bowling alleys but not for dining tables. Intimacy is encouraged when we are in proximity to the vibrations of human actions. To feel the laughter, to experience direct eye contact, and to be within earshot unite us. Large families should dine at round tables. Large gatherings should be set up with separate, more intimate tables.

Head tables at large events get the booby prize. Those long rectangular tables that seat diners like ducks all in a row provide an unpleasant dining experience.

If buying a new table is not an option, consider altering a table's shape by placing a round plywood circle atop the existing table. Although you may not be able to speak comfortably with all seated at a large round table, at least you are able to make enough eye contact to establish a feeling of connection.

If you have a cluttered dining area . . .

Just as it is better to eat slowly, allowing the body time to digest food properly, so it is better to subdue a room's stimulation. Create a peaceful, calm atmosphere that does not distract from digesting food or conversation. Relocate any extraneous furniture, art, and accessories to a room where stimulation is required.

If you don't have a light centered over the table . . .

If you would not read a book without adequate light illuminating the print, why would you eat without light shining on your food? Light is a way of emphasizing an important area. Without highlighting what is central, we may stray from the desired focus.

If an overhead light is not available, mount a spot on a nearby wall or position a floor lamp to shine on the table.

23

Kitchens

Even though it has been decades since I lived with my parents, the first thing I do when visiting them is check inside the refrigerator. On a deep level our relationship to food is so rudimentary that its association with life needs little substantiating. The kitchen is a place to feed our souls, bodies, and spirits; it should invoke reverence.

In producing good feng shui, yin and yang or balance is the condition for which we should strive. Although eating is essential to life and the kitchen is its vehicle, food is merely one of the major ingredients of life. We need to integrate the creation room for sustenance without unduly weighting its presence.

Test

Score 1 if the refrigerator is next to the stove.

Score 2 if a sink is in front of a window facing west.

Score 2 if a kitchen is seen when entering a home.

Score 1 if the stove and sink are very close together or very far apart.

SCORE 2 if you can't see the kitchen door from the most frequently used food preparation area.

SCORE 1 if the refrigerator is directly across from the entrance.

SCORE 2 if the kitchen is either too big or too small for the number of people who typically prepare the food.

SCORE 1 if the cooking utensils are inconveniently located.

SCORE 1 if the kitchen has no windows.

The total negative score could be 13. Naturally, curing all negative conditions is the ideal to strive toward. If you have scored almost one half of the total score, consider it a warning signal and attend to making some changes as soon as possible. Being surrounded by the best conditions helps you thrive!

If your refrigerator is next to the stove . . .

Like dropping an ice cub into a cup of scalding tea, hot in proximity to cold causes each essence to be diminished. Similarly, a refrigerator and stove require more energy to maintain their separate functions when they're too close together. When too much effort is needed to sustain essentials, the quality of life decreases.

The best cure for this situation is to reposition the refrigerator away from the stove. If this is impossible, buffer it with insulated material between the adjoining surfaces.

Refrigerators use a water element for cooling and a stove uses fire, so insert wood, the complementary element, in between. A tray or even a piece of cardboard can provide a symbolic buffer. Even one matchstick, according to Angel Thompson, a West Coast feng shui practitioner, will suffice.

If your sink is facing a western window . . .

Preparing a meal with the sun's setting rays directed in your face is like looking at an eclipse. Both cause potential damage. The daily job of preparing an evening meal should be conducted in a glare-free atmosphere.

Mitigate the harsh glare of the sun's setting rays by positioning plants or artifacts to filter the direct glare of the sun.

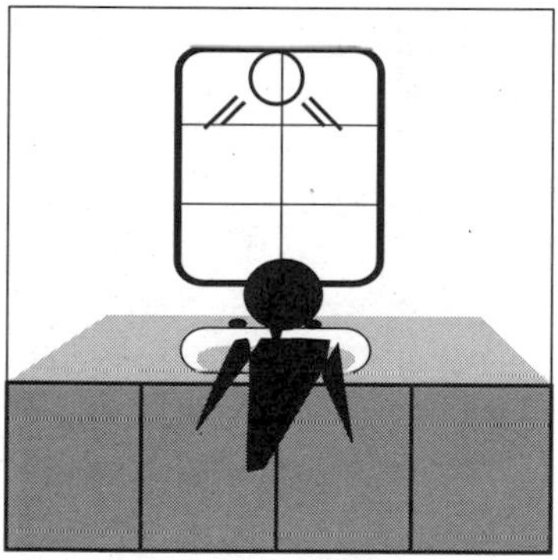

Cut the glare of the setting sun with plants or other objects in front of the window.

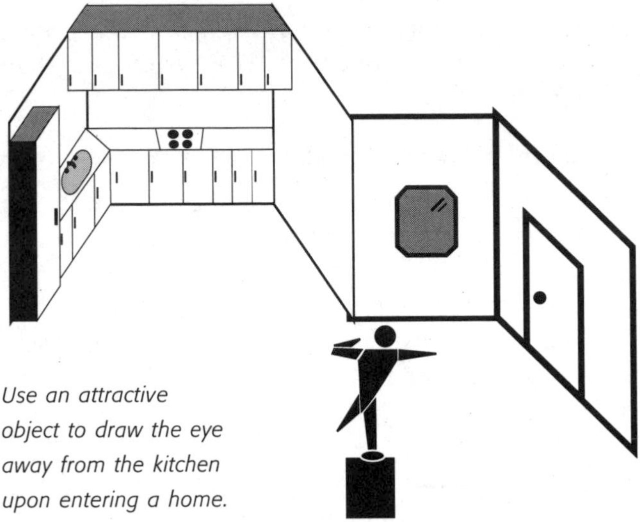

Use an attractive object to draw the eye away from the kitchen upon entering a home.

If your kitchen is close to the entrance of a home . . .

Sight, smell, and proximity to food are lures that few can ignore. Sometimes when I sit down to eat, I am not particularly hungry until the food is served. Then I become ravenous. We are influenced by what we see, and if the kitchen is close to a home's entrance, we might eat more than we need to.

Place a prominent object past the kitchen's entrance to attract attention elsewhere. By keeping a kitchen door closed and the lights off, we can similarly reduce the desire to enter.

If you have to take too many or too few steps between the stove and the sink . . .

While stove and sink need to be kept apart since fire and water are not auspicious next to each other, we need to keep them close enough together to expedite ease of food preparation. Carrying a boiling pot more than a few steps can be annoying and in some cases dangerous.

If the space between a stove and sink seems excessive, locate a chopping block or auxiliary table midway between the two. If floor space is too limited and the counter space is too great, keep a trivet midway between stove and sink. It will serve as a resting point on which to place pots filled to the brim.

If you are unable to see a kitchen's entrance when working at the stove . . .

To prepare nourishing foods, we need to immerse ourselves in the act of preparation. A centered level of concentration is required to complete this task successfully. Even Julia Child, who looks as if she is barely paying attention to the task at hand, is disguising a ferocious focus.

Feeling vulnerable or as if we could be taken by surprise undermines our concentration. Not seeing the door to a room in which we engage in activities that require concentration is detrimental to optimum performance.

Position a mirror to reflect the kitchen's entrance while working at the stove. Small convex mirrors designed for driveways and normally sold at hardware stores are ideal. If mirrors are not your cup of tea, mount a sound-producing object at the entrance to alert you when someone enters..

If the refrigerator is in direct line with the entrance door of the kitchen . . .

Retailers know the power of display and have lots of things for consumers to select while waiting at a checkout line. What we see is often what we want. Enter a gathering room and see a television set, and you'll probably turn it on. Enter a kitchen and see a refrigerator, and you may eat more.

Position a table piled high with distractions such as magazines, puzzles, or games between the refrigerator and the entrance. Any object that is positioned in the line of sight between the entrance and the refrigerator can serve as a momentary diversion to remind those entering to bypass eating.

Or conceal the refrigerator's shiny surface. Light reflecting off the shiny surface attracts the eye. Using Velcro to mount a piece of fabric on the door's surface is a simple way to cover a shiny, eye-catching refrigerator.

If you have a kitchen that is either too small or too large for the people who typically use it . . .

In Edward T. Hall's groundbreaking book on cultural distances, the *The Hidden Dimension*, there is a photograph of two women trying to cooking together in a narrow galley kitchen. You can tell that they cannot pass each other without bumping. The kitchen seems comical in proportion to the people who are using it.

On the other hand, a person working solo in a kitchen the size of Buckingham Palace conjures up another outlandish image. There must be a match between the size of a kitchen and the number of people who use it.

If a kitchen is too small, set up an auxiliary area to perform specific tasks. A dining table can serve as a salad preparation surface. Locate dishes and flatware in cabinets accessible to the dining table and out of the cooks' traffic pattern. Be inventive. A chest of drawers in the hallway next to a kitchen's door can be the perfect place to store dishes. Pots and pans hanging over a stove or against a wall can eliminate opening cupboards when more than one person is working in a tight area.

In an oversized area, when working alone, consolidate your most frequently used utensils to eliminate roaming all over the kitchen. A large plant, a massive ceramic bowl, music, and a swirling ceiling fan can all diminish the feeling of emptiness.

If you have a poorly organized kitchen . . .

Perhaps Julia Child would not let a five-minute hunt for a frying pan deter her from performing culinary miracles, but most of us find our energies sapped by the scourge of inconvenience.

Having to search through disorganized drawers and cupboards to uncover a needed utensil is maddening. Before I organized my spices on a rotating tray, I found myself losing patience when I had to search through an array of glass jars.

Organize kitchen paraphernalia for accessibility. Make sure staples are within easy reach. If cupboard space is lean, hang frequently used pots and pans to facilitate the preparation of food. Make life easy for yourself and find yourself whistling while you work.

If you have a kitchen without an outdoor view . . .

Although a restaurant's kitchen may function better without distractions, cooking at home is exalted by a feeling of connection. A windowless kitchen deprives the cook of connection with fresh air and sunlight. While we need to concentrate on the task at hand, feelings of isolation can be thwarted by a view outside.

If yours is a kitchen without windows, keep the entrance door to the kitchen open and position a plant, a fish tank, or any recirculating water outside. Plants unite us with the outside world. The sight of moving water contributes a soothing chi to the area, while the sound of water lessens the feeling of isolation.

If none of these cures is possible, use the color green in the kitchen. Green connects us subliminally to nature.

24

Bathrooms

Very few indoor spaces are designed to be used exclusively by one person at a time, and only with bathrooms is there a strong taboo against entering without permission. Because they are intended for private functions and we feel somewhat defenseless there, bathrooms should be partitioned off from activity rooms to ensure a feeling of seclusion. This works both ways: even hearing the sound of a flushing toilet or water draining from a bathroom sink can stir up uncomfortable feelings in those outside the bathroom, so it is best if bathroom sounds cannot be heard in a home's main rooms.

The contemporary expression "take a bath" implies a financial loss. In ancient China, water was a symbol for money, and a bathroom positioned by a front door signified the potential for loss. Whether we believe that water and money are synonymous, a bathroom is best positioned away from public rooms. When building a home, position closets, hallways, or staircases between a bathroom and the bedrooms, kitchen, or gathering rooms.

Test

Score 1 if a bathroom is near an entrance door.

Score 1 if a bathroom is directly off a gathering space.

SCORE 1 if the separate functions of a bathroom are not separated from each other when a bathroom is shared.

SCORE 2 if the toilet is directly in line with the bathroom entrance.

SCORE 1 for each bathroom door that opens outward.

SCORE 1 for each bathroom that has a common wall with a kitchen, a gathering room, or a bedroom.

The total negative score could be 7 or more. Naturally, curing all negative conditions is the ideal to strive toward. If you have scored almost one half of the total score, consider it a warning signal and attend to making some changes as soon as possible. Being surrounded by the best conditions helps you thrive!

If you have a bathroom near a home's entrance . . .

My husband and I often travel by car to vacation spots. Inevitably we have to make a pit stop. If we can't find an appropriate roadside rest area, we look for a convenient restaurant. Finding a place with a bathroom posi-

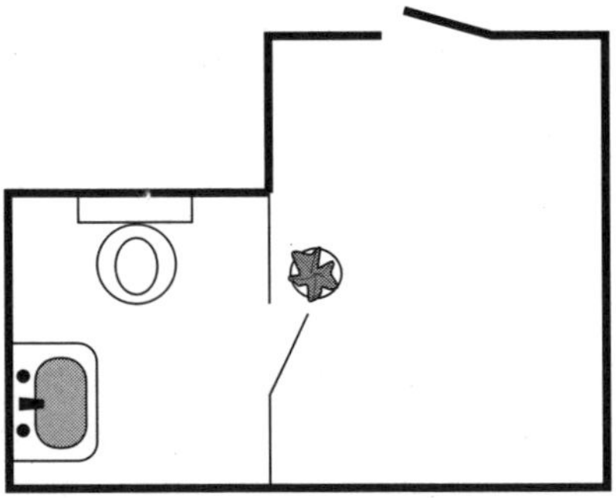

Block a view of the bathroom from an entrance with a strategically placed plant or screen.

tioned by an entrance door makes us feel less guilty about using the bathroom without patronizing the restaurant. While public facilities often position bathrooms near the door to discourage guests from walking through busy areas, there's no such need in a home.

First impressions are duplicated on some level every time we enter a space, and being greeted by a bathroom does not usually telegraph the highest and best message.

Create a feeling of separation between a bathroom and an entrance. If space permits, place a plant, screen, or sculpture as a divider before the door. If there is not enough room, hang a mirror on the bathroom door to help it disappear.

Paint the inside of the bathroom door a darker color than the foyer. A deep color will make the bathroom's interior recede. The fragrance of mint or pine can add to a feeling of separation. A secure visible lock and a stash of extra toilet tissues under the sink adds to the feeling of privacy.

If a bathroom opens into a main room . . .

In my book, *Designing Your Happiness*, I tell the story of a neighborhood Thanksgiving dinner in a home that had only one bathroom located directly off the party area. One guest was so mortified at having to pass in front of all the dinner guests to enter the bathroom that she left the party and went home to use her own bathroom.

A bathroom should be partitioned off, buffered by sound and sight, from communal spaces. We tend to feel constrained using a bathroom when we know people are seated right outside the door. It seems to be a fairly common practice for restaurants to screen rest rooms that open directly into a dining space. Why then do so many builders position bathrooms to open directly in line with seating or sleeping areas?

Since it is unlikely that you will change the location of the bathroom and in some cases cannot change the location of a bed or seating unit, partitioning off the toilet area from view is the best alternative. If the bathroom is too small or configured in such a way as to make adding anything inside impossible, then either place a high piece of furniture against the adjacent room's wall or hang a large painting, poster, padded fabric, or any wall covering that thickens the feeling of the wall.

If a bathroom is not partitioned to separate the toilet from other areas . . .

Even in small bathrooms you can generate a feeling of separation for each function. Positioning a plant, screen, or curtain to partition the toilet from other areas can provide a sense of privacy.

Recently I've noticed that builders are starting to separate the toilet from the sink and tub area. I consider that a positive trend, but remember that any feng shui

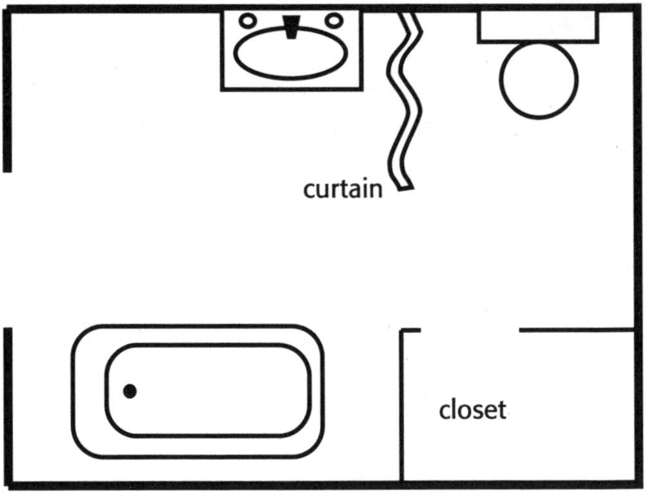

Partition the bathroom for its separate functions.

application has to resonate with culture and personal preferences. In many homes, partners share the same bathroom and need to use it at the same time. While this is not ideal, it is reality for many and we need to deal with it. In the best-case scenario, the toilet will be separated into another room with its own door; the alternative is to provide some sort of visual barrier. For those who feel bathroom functions need no more privacy than watching TV, cures are not needed.

If your bathroom door opens with a view of the toilet . . .

Front and center is the perfect position for a royal seat but not for a throne in a bathroom. A toilet should be tucked behind a door, wall, or cabinet. If changing the location of the toilet is impossible and the space is too small to curtain it off, the best alternative is to position seating in the adjacent room so there is no view of the bathroom door. If that is impossible, at least provide the occupant of a bathroom with a hook and eye, sliding bolt, or any visible latch to lock the bathroom door. Seeing a lock instead of trusting a hidden lock mechanism gives the occupant a greater feeling of security.

If your bathroom's door opens out . . .

When a door swings to the outside of a room, the interior is totally visible. The bathroom is not a room whose innards we want to expose.

If the door cannot be rehung, secure a curtain inside the doorjamb for privacy. If a curtain is unacceptable in your decorating scheme and the room is large enough, place a plant to block the greatest view to the inside.

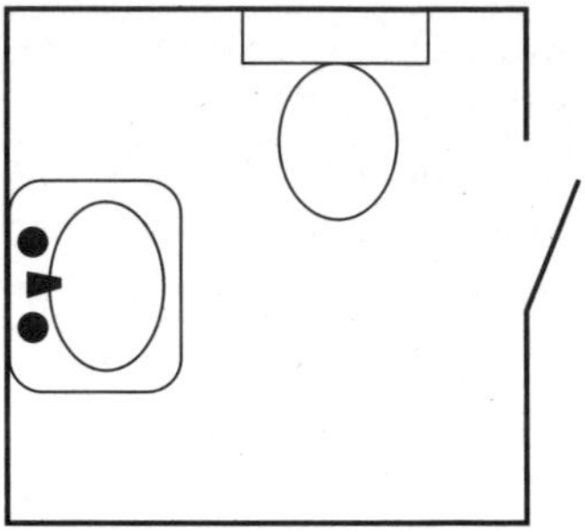

An outward-opening door reveals a room that should remain private.

If your bathroom has a common wall with a kitchen, bedroom, dining room, or gathering room . . .

I have seen homes with a main bedroom separated from a bathroom by a wall that does not reach the ceiling. Normally the wall is eight feet high, but the common ceiling is peaked so airspace is shared between the two rooms. The magic of a marriage might drift away when a bedroom's airspace is shared with that of a bathroom.

If a bathroom shares a wall with a bedroom or a public room, create an additional buffer between these two areas by placing a cabinet or bookcase against the common wall. If furniture is not appropriate, hang a painting or mirror to form a barrier separating these two rooms. We feel more secure when we are buffeted by layers.

25

Bedrooms

A bedroom is a sanctuary to house our most private dreams and thoughts as well as an enclosure providing our body an opportunity to rejuvenate. By honoring this space we are honoring our own uniqueness.

A main function of the bedroom is to provide a haven for relaxation and sleep. On the deepest level we need to feel shielded from unwanted surprises, whether it's a child bounding in to wake us up or the dreaded burglar in the night. We need to see those entering our space at least at the same time as they see us.

A bedroom should feel private. Often a closet separates the bedroom from other rooms. Our own reading light can give a feeling of solitude even when this space is shared.

A bedroom should also allow us the necessary transition time from dreaming to reality. Seeing a desk piled high with papers or our reflection in a mirror upon awakening can cause too abrupt a passage from sleep to wakefulness.

Test

Score 1 for each bed in direct line with an entrance door.

Score 2 if an entrance door is either behind you or out of convenient sight while you're in bed.

SCORE 1 if a mirror is in direct view when you arise.

SCORE 1 if an open door hides a bed from view.

SCORE 1 if the head and one side of a double bed occupied by two persons are against walls.

SCORE 2 if you can see a toilet from bed when a bathroom door is open.

SCORE 1 if your bed is against a wall in common with a bathroom.

SCORE 2 if a work area is visible either when you're entering a bedroom or when you're in bed.

SCORE 1 if the majority of your bed is in front of a window.

SCORE 2 if the head of a bed has no wall behind it.

SCORE 1 if you sleep underneath a prominent beam.

SCORE 2 if a bedroom is off the entrance foyer of a home.

The total negative score could be 17. Naturally, curing all negative conditions is the ideal to strive toward. If you have scored almost one half of the total score, consider it a warning signal and attend to making some changes as soon as possible. Being surrounded by the best conditions helps you thrive!

If your bed is in line with an entrance door . . .

When we are directly across from an entrance we are more vulnerable because we are easily seen by those

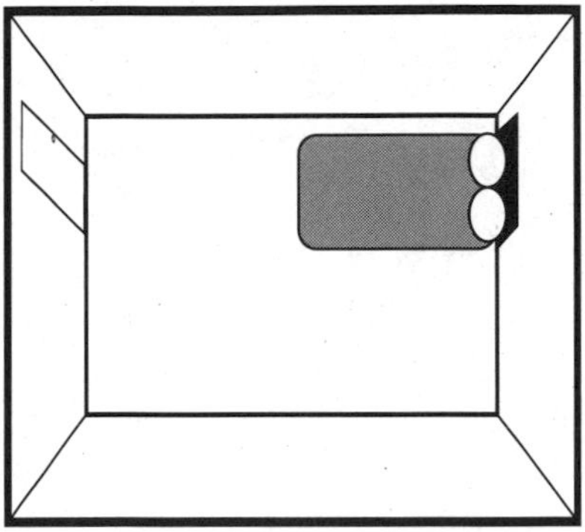

A bed directly across from the door leaves us feeling too exposed.

entering. Being off to one side gives us more time to react to anyone entering.

If there is no other place for a bed except on a wall in direct line with an entrance door, position a movement-sensitive object outside or on the bedroom door to produce a sound that can be heard when someone approaches.

If you can't see a bedroom's entrance from bed without having to rotate your head more than thirty degrees . . .

To rejuvenate our physical and mental processes, we need to be able to relax completely. Whether reading, resting, or sleeping, not seeing the door into the bedroom can make the difference between feeling completely relaxed and feeling slightly on edge.

In most cases moving the bed to grant a view of an entrance is all that is necessary. If that is not possible, place a mirror across from the bed to reflect the door. Make sure the mirror is not in a direct line with the bed. (See next cure for details.)

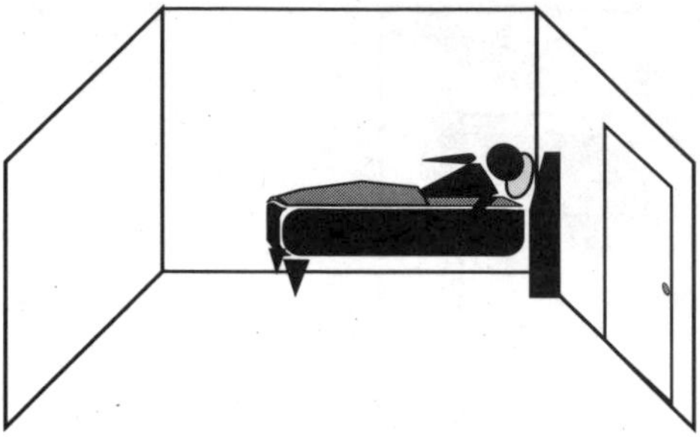

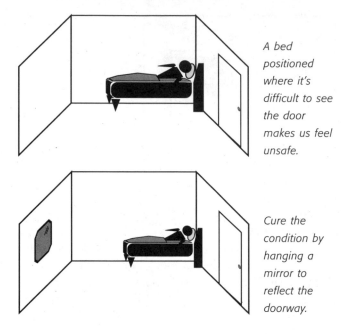

A bed positioned where it's difficult to see the door makes us feel unsafe.

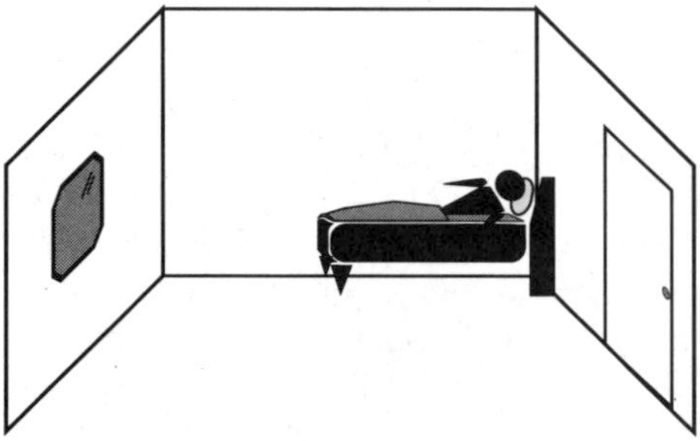

Cure the condition by hanging a mirror to reflect the doorway.

If a mirror is positioned so that you see yourself while sitting in bed or as soon as you get up . . .

The state of transition from sleep to wakefulness is fragile. Our waking moments should gently connect us to our surroundings, perhaps by our seeing a loved one's face, hearing nature's sounds, or seeing a treasured artifact.

A mirror in which you see yourself immediately upon waking is not a good idea because most of us are critical of our image. My morning look includes tousled hair and yesterday's eye makeup smeared on my cheeks. Only when I have completed my bathroom rituals and righted the night's assault do I care to venture a peep at myself.

Replace any mirror that can be seen when first waking up with a painting, poster, or tapestry.

If your bed is hidden by an opening door . . .

When a bed is tucked away behind an open door, the person entering is screened. At first you might feel protected from being seen in a compromising situation, but remember, if they can't see you, you can't see them.

Position a mirror in such a way as to reveal the person entering.

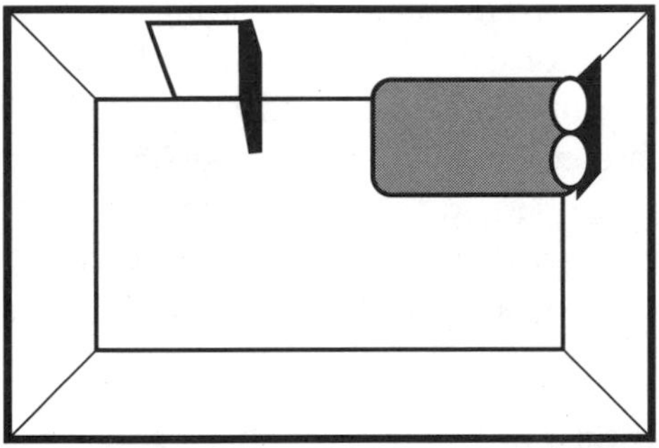

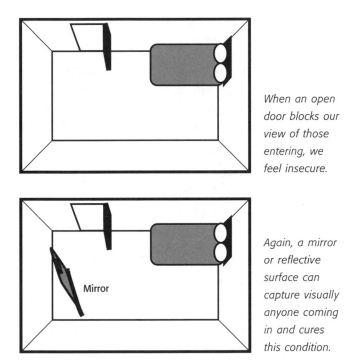

When an open door blocks our view of those entering, we feel insecure.

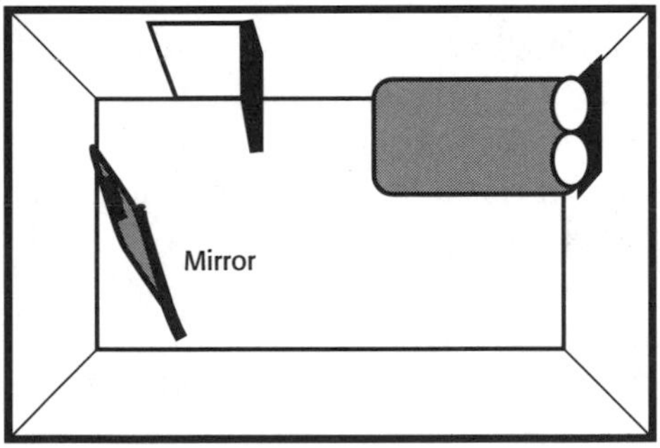

Again, a mirror or reflective surface can capture visually anyone coming in and cures this condition.

If you have a double bed up against two walls . . .

When a double bed for two people is up against two walls, one person cannot get up easily. Climbing over a bed mate or scooting down to the foot of a bed to rise feels awkward. The confined bed mate finds his or her chi stymied and can feel as if his or her aspirations are impeded by obstacles.

No matter how tiny the surrounding space, be sure to position a double bed with three sides away from a wall. If this is impossible, consider getting a smaller bed or moving the sleeping area to another part of the home.

If there is a toilet in direct view from bed . . .

American culture has strong taboos supporting utter privacy for toilet functions. Seeing a toilet is similar to watching someone burping, so move chairs and beds out of view of a bathroom door. If this is impossible, hang a curtain across the doorjamb so that the curtain is not affected when the door opens. When these options are not acceptable, position a screen to create a foyer before the bathroom.

If your bed is against a wall common with a bathroom . . .

Early Chinese plumbing was rarely completely sealed, and gases emitted as a by-product of human waste could be harmful. With today's pristine plumbing we worry less about those health risks, but bathroom sounds still should not be heard in sleeping areas. Unfortunately, master bathrooms in bedrooms make this difficult to avoid. If your master bedroom is configured this way, at least try not to place the bed against the shared wall; also read the last cure in Chapter 24.

If there is no other position for a bed, hang a tapestry, a plaque, or any thick wall hanging to muffle and buffer the wall separating the bedroom and bathroom.

If a work area is visible upon your entering a bedroom or while in bed . . .

Reminders of obligations can undermine our ability to rest. Surely if the last thing you see each night or the first thing you see in the morning is a desk with its conspicuous reminders of pending labors, the prospect of tranquility is more remote. Life should be a feast, and each course should be served separately.

Position a screen or plant to conceal a work area in a bedroom. It matters less what the shielding item is so long as it is something that resonates with the room's aesthetics.

If your bed is placed in front of a window or without a wall behind it . . .

A window behind a bed exposes us in the same way as a door directly across from a bed does. Deep relaxation is not enhanced by knowing we could be taken by surprise.

A bed needs a solid wall behind it to feel backed and supported. Placing a bed in the center of a room does nothing to quell our need to feel safe from predators.

If there is no other location for the bed, be sure to close the window's covering before retiring. For those who don't like curtains, consider suspending a painting or plaque within the frame of the window. Position a mirror to reflect the scene behind the bed if the head of a bed needs to remain facing away from an entrance door.

If there is a beam directly over a sleeping area . . .

In the days when humans had little but intelligence and guts to ward off predators, few things were more menacing than being attacked from above. We feel unsafe when exposed and unprotected if we're underneath anything that could pose a threat. A beam over a sleeping area undermines complete rest because of this ancient memory.

Ancient feng shui tells us that the part of a body over which a beam passes will be prone to illness. Therefore, if an overhead beam crosses over your midsection, you might have digestive problems. The part of your body over which a beam passes may tense or retract because of the experiential weight of an overhead beam.

If you live in an earthquake-prone area, reposition the bed out from under a beam.

In areas not subject to earthquakes or mud slides, mirroring the underside of the beam, making it visually disappear, will render a beam innocuous.

If you have a bedroom off an entrance foyer . . .

A bedroom near an entrance door lures the room's occupants to cloister themselves in their personal space instead of joining family members in a gathering space. In the case of an adult living alone, a bedroom near the entrance may encourage a desire to lie down and perhaps be lazy instead of being motivated to engage in other activities.

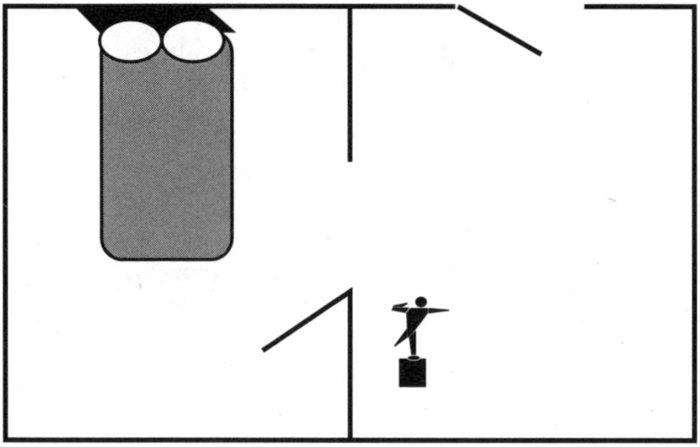

Positioning an object to draw attention away from a bedroom door keeps people entering the home moving into its main gathering space.

Moreover, a bedroom positioned near a front entrance is likely to feel less safe and more invaded by public space, especially if the front faces a street.

If there are no options to change the bedroom's position, try these remedies:

- Keep the door to the bedroom closed.
- Position another object that has a strong compelling positive image at the far side of the bedroom door.

For example, a bookcase positioned to the far side of the door can remind us of the pleasures of reading. A photograph of other family members can strike a chord of family unity. In both cases we are pulled toward the heart of a home by the position of a stimulating object.

26

WORK SPACES

I passed on to my children the knowledge that all things can be accomplished with focus. Whether we concentrate better in a blue room or an orange room, with or without music, or looking over an energy-driven or tranquil atmosphere, the central consideration is to create an atmosphere that supports our unique needs.

Be it a place to focus on a job, hobby, or household chore a home's work spaces should be honored and supported with the best conditions.

TEST

SCORE 2 if a work space is in an out-of-the-way or undesirable location.

SCORE 2 if you feel isolated and unconnected while at your workstation.

SCORE 2 if you work in a windowless office.

SCORE 2 if you feel uncomfortable because of the number of people sharing your work space.

SCORE 2 if you cannot see the entrance door while working.

SCORE 1 if your work space is contiguous to a kitchen.

SCORE 1 if your work space is contiguous to a bathroom.

SCORE 1 if a heating or air-conditioning duct is above your chair.

SCORE 1 if you cannot see the door while talking on the telephone.

SCORE 2 if light comes in over the shoulder of your writing hand.

SCORE 1 if your workstation is next to the exit door.

SCORE 2 if a secret arrow is pointing at your workstation. (Refer to Chapter 14.)

The total negative score could be 19. Naturally, curing all negative conditions is the ideal to strive toward. If you have scored almost one half of the total score, consider it a warning signal and attend to making some changes as soon as possible. Being surrounded by the best conditions helps you thrive!

If your work space is in an inappropriate or out-of-the-way location . . .

When I was making a living as an artist, I delivered a sculpture to a client. This couple proudly gave me a tour of their home. Opening the door to what I was told was his office revealed a bathroom! I knew it was no joke after seeing a desk squeezed into a corner. Questioning him revealed that his selection was based on the guaranteed privacy this room afforded. Legitimate reason but horrible feng shui.

We become what is anticipated. Don't squeeze a desk into a corner of a room or stash it in a windowless basement. The quality of work will mirror the status of the work space.

This doesn't mean that a work space in a garage might not be just what you need. Middle-of-the-night flashes of inspiration might be best executed in a space away from the main household. A work space is appropriate when it cradles you and at the same time gives you emotional, mental, and physical support. Whatever form it takes, having a quality place in which to concentrate on doing a job well is an element that holds together a fulfilling life.

If you feel isolated and unconnected while at your work station . . .

While we need privacy, we do not like to feel isolated. Finding the right mix of privacy and connectedness is like seasoning food—the individual must be savvy about the palate and alert to the alterations the spices may make. While some people use a photograph of loved ones to feel connected, others use music or a radio talk show to provide a background that nurtures a sense of well-being. The best link to the outside world is personal. Make a decision to have something in your work space that reminds you of the benefits of the other parts of your life.

If you work in a windowless office . . .

Without a connection to the outside world, we feel confined as if in prison. Workers in windowless offices suffer unending low-level anxiety and feel as if they are missing out on life. Dissatisfaction with your job is likely to surface when you're surrounded by only walls.

If your workroom is windowless, introduce a chi-engaging object. It might be as simple as a photograph of a favorite vacation spot, a small assortment of shells collected during a summer vacation, or a paper mobile hanging under a duct that blows air or as elaborate as an indoor recirculating fountain, a wall mural of a nature scene, or a swirling ceiling fan. Choose something that links you to the vitality and energy outside.

If you feel uncomfortable because of the number of people in the same space . . .

You may be the type to feel energized by mobs of people, or you may be intimidated by a crush of humanity. Either way, being in the midst of what feels like too many people can rob you of your personal resolve.

A screen can be physical or emotional. To prevent a loss of personal identity or a feeling of being overwhelmed, create another focus. A spotlight to pool a personal space, a soundproofing partition, or a basket of flowers can override the hubbub of working in a highly charged space.

I once shared an office with a woman who wore a deep brimmed hat. It flopped over her eyes and provided her with a screen of privacy. Whether eccentric or not, find a way of defining your personal space.

If you are unable to see an entrance door while working . . .

My mom almost never forgave her older sister for terrorizing her while they were growing up. Aunt Betty would stand behind a door waiting for my mother to pass by, then jump out and yell, "Boo!" No one likes to be startled, and that's exactly what can happen if someone can come from behind before you realize they are there.

The easiest and most effective way to cure this situation, short of repositioning the furniture, is to place a mirror so that you can look up and see the reflection of the door without having to turn around. If you work on a computer, get some putty and stick a small pocket mirror on the side of the monitor. Make it easy, make it simple; just be able to see the door.

If you have a workroom contiguous to a kitchen or bathroom . . .

My kitchen is a short four steps below my office. When frustrated, anxious about a project, or just plain tired, I find myself mysteriously gravitating toward the refrigerator. Sometimes I catch myself while I am poised on step three and turn back to my office. Food, the stuff of life, often becomes a pacifier for angst and a diversion from problem solving. If you are too close to a kitchen, you may end up carrying around unresolved work problems and extra weight.

If moving to another location far from the kitchen is not an option, create a barrier from the sounds, smells, and thoughts of eating. Hang a tapestry or carpet on the contiguous wall to absorb the sounds. Light a bayberry candle or mist the air with a flowered fragrance to camouflage the smells. A picture of a favored sport or beach scene can remind you of the benefits of being fit and healthy.

An adage that comes to my mind when I find myself drifting to the kitchen is "Half the time you think you're hungry, you're really only thirsty." Therefore, my bottle of Evian water is always close by.

If a heating or air-conditioning duct is directly over a workstation . . .

Sitting under forced air heating ducts will lull the senses like a pile of blankets protecting you from a winter's chill. On the other hand, a cold draft from the same duct in summertime can make you recede like a turtle into its shell. In either case, your optimal performance is hindered by the breadth of extremes.

When unable to move yourself out from under a heating and cooling duct, try hanging a scarf, an umbrella, or an art object under the duct to help deflect the draft away from you. At the very least, turn the vent slats to one side so that the air doesn't blow directly downward.

If you cannot see the door while on the telephone . . .

Old movies often show a critical piece of information being revealed to the wrong person because someone talking on the phone does not see the person eavesdropping by the door. Evil triumphs because the telephone is positioned with bad feng shui. Why take a chance that you could be overheard when talking on the telephone? Free yourself from any concerns other than conducting business. View the entrance door while using the telephone.

If a direct view of the door is not possible, position a mirror to reflect the door. If you have a spectacular view and want to look out the window when speaking on the phone, have either a wind-sensitive object or a bell on the door to indicate someone has crossed the threshold.

If light falls across your dominant hand . . .

We need to eliminate as many distractions as possible to focus on a task. Not even a shadow should come between you and your work. Any encumbrance lessens your effectiveness.

If light shines over the shoulder of your writing hand, a shadow will fall across the working surface. If light comes from the side unobstructed by a hand, the surface will be without shadows. Shadows sap you of direct focus for the task at hand.

Position a light above or on the side of the nondominant hand. I have perched a light atop my computer to shine directly down on my keyboard, leaving me a working surface free of distractions.

If you have a workstation next to the room's exit door . . .

The worst table in a restaurant is the one right next to the door. Few like to be near any door, be it the kitchen door or the one to the rest rooms. If your work station is close to an exit door, you might be viewed by those coming through the door as a dispensable part and treated as such. So if you don't want your mate or children to interrupt you, place a work area away from the entrance door of a room.

If changing locations is not an option, place a heavy, colorful object, a wind-sensitive item, or a sound producing mechanism on the side of the desk close to the door. Anytime someone passes by, you will be noticed. Adding chi to your presence will add importance to your role, for both yourself and those who work with you.

The Cures

Special Considerations

27

FURNITURE

Furniture defines a room's use and should fit the dimensions of a space. A room should be neither jammed nor empty.

Furniture determines how we move through space. It should further the room's intent as well as the traffic patterns for the entire home. Consider these questions before selecting the amount and placement of furniture for any room:

- What kind of activities do I want this room to promote?
- How many people will typically use it?
- Which rooms need to be connected easily to each other?
- At what time of day will this room be used most frequently?

TEST

SCORE 2 if you have to squeeze by to access any piece of furniture.

SCORE 1 if the room feels too empty of furniture.

SCORE 2 if the main seating in a room has its back to the most frequently used entrance door.

SCORE 2 if there are too few seats for the number of people who typically use a room.

SCORE 2 if you have to walk more than eight or ten steps into a room prior to sitting down.

The total negative score could be 9. Naturally, curing all negative conditions is the ideal to strive toward. If you have scored almost one half of the total score, consider it a warning signal and attend to making some changes as soon as possible. Being surrounded by the best conditions helps you thrive!

If a room has too much furniture . . .

Many studies test the results of overcrowding on the human condition. Edward T. Hall, in his book *The Silent Language*, reports that our reproductive capacity changes in relation to the number of people per square foot. Emotional responses like anger, anxiety, and fear are closer to the surface whenever density exceeds a certain limit.

We must create an appropriate balance between too much stimulus and too little, and there is no substitute for weeding out what is unnecessary. A good rule of thumb for seating is to have about two to four more seats than the number of people who typically use an area.

Crammed-full cabinets often represent an inability to change. One of my students once told me a story about her grandmother. Whenever she asked her grandmother a question, her grandmother would tell her, "Go up to your room and empty one dresser drawer." Decide what is really needed and put back only the things you will use." Inevitably, before she had completed the task, the answer to her question popped into her head. Her grandmother knew that you can't receive information until you clear a space for it.

If a room has too little furniture . . .

Although there are situations when sparseness is appropriate, most of us need a complex environment in which to thrive. Stimulation provides the catalyst for stretching our mental processes. Studies describe how infants waste away in a world devoid of stimuli. When left exclusively to their own devices, these children become morose and withdraw from the world physically and emotionally.

The artist Georgia O'Keeffe threw white sheets over all her furniture in her all-white studio. This pristine environment provided the necessary backdrop for the vivid colors of her paintings to stand out like a tree's silhouette on a snow-covered landscape. For most of us, however, details and colors provide a springboard for creativity.

If your purpose is truly assisted by empty space, then by all means don't change it. However, if you are not providing appropriate stimulation in your environment, increase the objects, color, or light.

I once visited a student who craved visual splendor but whose pocketbook could not meet those demands. Her solution was ingenious. She cut out different pictures and pasted them on cardboard and hung them in an Andy Warhol fashion on her walls. In this case, invention is the mother of success. Never say, "I don't have. . . ." Look around for an idea waiting to be born.

Displaying pictures is a possible cure for a room that lacks stimulation.

If a sofa or the main seating units in a room face away from the room's entrance door . . .

Any place of contemplation or concentration should support a feeling of complete contentment. To feel safe we need to see who's approaching. If not, we are unconsciously attuned to slight sounds, physical vibrations, or air currents. This prevents us from being in the moment.

Position a main seating area to face the room's most frequently used entrance. When this is not possible, position a mirror to reflect the entrance.

If there are too few seating units for the number of people who typically use a room . . .

A family with three teenage sons sought my help when, after moving into their dream home, they found their family unity dissipating. They had moved from a small home that had one large gathering room to a big home with a huge formal gathering room and a tiny family gathering room.

Two couches filled up the entire floor space in their informal gathering space, but no more than four sprawling young males could sit down comfortably. Their sons ended up entertaining their friends apart from the family, and their family cohesion was disrupted. The culprit was insufficient seating space for the number of people.

I suggested changing the large formal area into the family area but was fought tooth and nail. Their sons lost out to the parents' desire for a magazine-dream-inspired home.

If you have to walk more than eight or ten steps into a room before you can sit down . . .

Very few of us like to listen to a speaker who rambles. When I am listening to someone so inclined, I hear myself mentally saying, "Get to the point." In the same way, a room should get to the point. Its focus should be within a reasonable distance of its entrance. Even though "too far" is a relative term, I would suggest you determine whether the heart of a room is outside a comfortable distance to traverse. If it is, the remedy is to provide an alternative stopping off place, and in many cases that would be a seat or seating unit within the first ten paces into a room.

28

LIGHT

Surrounded by a carload of buddies describing what was ahead, which way to turn the wheel, and when to apply the brakes, my children's blind friend realized a life's dream and drove a car. Certainly those who have lost their sight develop compensating skills in sometimes remarkable ways. However, our ability to discern what we need to know is diminished dramatically if we are unable to see clearly.

TEST

SCORE 2 if there is only overhead lighting in a room.

SCORE 2 for all areas that do not have sufficient lighting.

SCORE 2 if a reading chair or a desk does not have a pool of light surrounding it.

SCORE 1 for any indoor or outdoor lighting shining in your eyes.

SCORE 2 for any room without natural lighting.

The total negative score could be 9 or more. Naturally, curing all negative conditions is the ideal to strive toward. If you have scored almost one half of the total score, consider it a warn-

ing signal and attend to making some changes as soon as possible. Being surrounded by the best conditions helps you thrive!

If there is no variation of light in a room . . .

The light inside a home should approximate, as closely as possible, the variety and intensity of sunlight. It feels normal to enter consciousness each morning with streaks of light low on the horizon lifting the veil of night. During the rest of the day light often peers through trees or is punctuated by clouds rolling by. Light is rarely unrelenting—as it feels in a room with nothing but overhead lighting—but rather is textured with shadows and gradations of bright and dim. It behooves us to replicate these conditions.

Provide area lighting in conjunction with overall lighting in any room. For example, in an office graced with nothing more than overhead fluorescent lighting, install desk lamps to project cones of light over a work area.

If there is not enough light . . .

I always thought one childhood friend had a most peculiar home. After the sun went down, the family played tag with the home's illumination. When walking upstairs, you were required to shut the lights off on the floor below and vice versa on the return trip. There was always a black hole following you around the house. Who knew what was lurking behind? Darkness obscures visibility, and when we can't see we often feel uneasy. Biology has programmed us to use our sight as an important tool. Our eyes are first in a line of defense systems necessary for survival.

Install two kinds of lighting systems, one that illuminates all areas in a general way and another to highlight specific areas. Be creative: purchase a socket and cord and feed it through a flexible copper tube sitting in a chunk of wood and top it off with a clip-on shade. Lighting can be as expensive or reasonably priced as you like.

If you are not framing important areas . . .

Light is associated with awareness, wisdom, and freedom. It is no coincidence that angels are encircled in light. Being excluded from inside the cone of light is to be viewed as less significant. Expressions such as "outside the limelight" and "shadowy figure" all indicate our positive association with light. We find people bathed in light more believable and more desirable than those who are not.

If a cone of light fails to include the entire conversation area or cuts a person sitting on the sofa in half, reposition the light. To make the person feel included in an activity and to encourage productivity, frame the complete person within the sphere of light.

Illuminate all spaces appropriately. Consider where the circle of light falls and be sure all seating is appropriately contained within its cone.

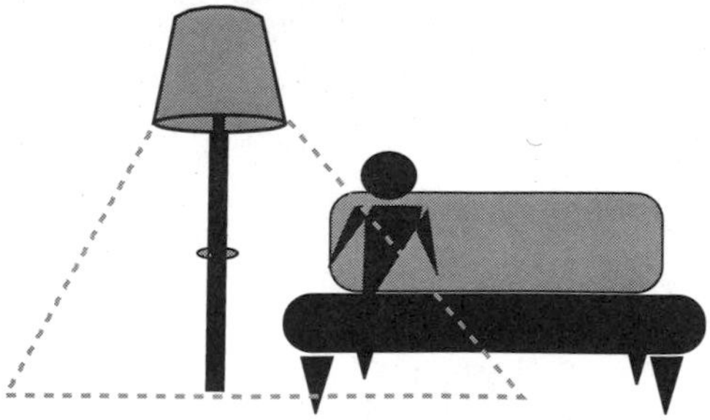

Lights form pools that should encompass, not cut in half, a person sitting nearby.

If you have lighting that shines in a person's eyes . . .

Police tactics in old movies sometimes include intermittently flashing a bright light in a suspect's face. It momentarily confuses the suspect because while eyes adjust instantly to bright light, it takes longer to adjust to darkness. The cumulative effect is a blurring of the surrounding scene, rendering the suspect vulnerable and hence more likely to lose the resolve to remain silent.

Adjust all lighting in such a way as to avoid any direct beam of light aimed toward a person's eyes.

If a room is devoid of natural light . . .

The windowless room, an environment many modern-day office workers deal with, can be cured in many ways. First of all, purchase full-spectrum lightbulbs, which today are manufactured even for fluorescent light fixtures. Full-spectrum light has all the colors within its spectrum and thus duplicates sunlight most closely.

Make sure to have a depth view such as a landscape, street, or other subject in which you see a distant perspective via a photograph, picture, or calendar. Looking beyond four walls if only through an artist's representation is better than being visually stymied by the edges of a windowless room.

Any representation of nature, such as an indoor fountain, fish tank, or plant, can help remove the claustrophobic feeling of a windowless room.

29

MOVEMENT

Nothing in nature is static. Even rocks are boiling vats of moving molecules. A slab of glass stored vertically will thicken at the lower end over time because glass, like all things, is in perpetual motion.

Movement attracts attention. In the very first days of life an infant's involuntary eye response establishes a lifetime connection between action and life. On an emotional level inaction makes us feel devoid of contact. Even for those who spurn busy, bustling environments, this primal association makes us relate positively toward movement.

Doldrums are weather patterns devoid of air currents. To be in a doldrum is to be listless and lack energy. The absence of air currents is equated with what's lackluster in life because movement is part and parcel of every living thing's experience. To be without an awareness of things in motion is to live outside life's normal parameters.

TEST

SCORE 2 for each room that feels too still.

SCORE 1 for each area that feels too frenetic.

If one third of the entire living space feels too still or too frenetic, consider installing feng shui cures.

If your home is too still . . .

Don't confuse stillness with quiet. Stillness includes the absence of movement and sound, while quiet conjures up peacefulness. Rocking in a hemp hammock on a summer's day soothes us in much the same way as a cradle lulls an infant to sleep. Movement is seen, felt, and heard in the natural world in every setting. A wisp of snow moving across the ground, the ridge of a receding wave, and a butterfly fluttering over a garden are all familiar sights in our shifting world.

Too much stillness leaves us fragile and sometimes morose. As pets are routinely eliminated by the rules of condominium complexes and retirement communities and living spaces are superinsulated, preventing air from moving freely through an environment, dwellings for single citizens are becoming stagnant and funereal. Quiet is a tapering of stimuli, while stillness is its absence.

Being engaged in any activity quells stillness. The bubbling of a small recirculating fountain, plants with small lightweight leaves that are apt to rustle when someone passes by, and fluffy pillows that squash delightfully when leaned against provide different kinds of movement.

One of my favorite cures for homes of single dwellers is to mount a small fan at the base of a small-leafed plant to promote fluttering of its leaves. It provides a delightful antidote to stillness.

If your home has too much motion . . .

In 1950s movies madness was often represented by photographing the drama inside a person's head. Images would float strobe-like across the screen, and the wretched victim would be helpless to screen out the stimuli. There was no escape from insanity in the realm of stimulation overload.

The heart and soul of life lie in balancing all stimuli. Procuring enough activity to stimulate appropriately while eliminating extraneous distractions produces the best environment.

Movement can be controlled in most situations. When it can't, however, human beings seem to have an innate coping mechanism. Tony Hiss, in his book *Experience of Place*, observes the way crowds move through Manhattan's Grand Central Station. Even when the central room is filled to capacity, none of the thousands of people collide. For the most part humans have an ability to orchestrate their movements appropriately. Only the element of panic seems to undermine harmonious interactions.

When restraining movement is out of your control, make the space appear as large as possible. Perhaps it is time to throw away any extra furniture or repaint a room a lighter, brighter color. Mirrors, reflecting a calm scene outside a window or even an unadorned wall, often help a space seem larger. Highlight the area you use with additional wattage. A pool of light over your chair can help cocoon you from distractions.

If none of these suggestions can be implemented easily, try hanging a small sculpture, a painting, or any object near the ceiling. This object should be easy to see and will serve to lift visual attention over areas and give a room's occupants a reference point for concentration. If an appropriate item cannot be found, paint a stripe at the juncture of the wall and ceiling to divert attention away from the frenetic area.

30

Rituals

It may be a morning stretch, a glass of lemon water, or merely tooth brushing, but the odds are good you begin each day with some routine. A ritual is nothing more than an established procedure. Rituals can be as mundane as a trip to the bathroom or as uncommon as standing on your head. In any case, rituals are anchors to experience.

We find it surprising when someone does not celebrate a birthday, anniversary, or occasional holiday. In addition to these customary events, there are uniquely personal ones, a first day at a job or the day we move into a new home. These experiences are so central to life's overall evolution that they demand commemoration with ceremony.

Acknowledging the completion of one cycle before we begin another is a way to honor the past even though we are moving on. The day I left for college, unbeknown to my parents, I put a lucky penny under our doormat. It was my way of leaving something at home while trusting to the fortunes of my future. Breaking open a bottle of favored liquor to toast a beginning or burning sage to purify and sanctify a new home is life affirming. Rituals link the passage of time in a way that honors both the past and the future.

TEST

SCORE 2 if you haven't any special days that commemorate a personal event.

SCORE 2 if you change homes without connecting the change with a ritual.

The total negative score could be 4. Naturally, curing all negative conditions is the ideal to strive toward. If you have scored one half of the total score, consider it a warning signal and attend to making some changes as soon as possible. Being surrounded by the best conditions helps you thrive!

If you do not celebrate special days commemorating personal events . . .

Those who do not treat themselves as special are also likely to subjugate their uniqueness. To achieve, we need to feel special. Whether it be our talents, our family, or merely our being alive, separating ourselves to bestow attention and esteem is one way of augmenting the fulfillment of a positive destiny.

Most parents would not dare miss a child's birthday, because to do so is sending a negative message to that child. Even for adults, displaying self-love is a positive reinforcer of self-esteem, and one way to express self-love is to celebrate distinctly personal events.

Pick a day, any day, and celebrate you. If you are not a birthday kind of person, here are some suggestions.

- The day you started your job
- The day you met your beloved
- The day you ran a marathon

- The day you moved into your home
- The day your child graduated from high school
- The day you won an award
- The day you went to (fill in the place)
- The day you joined (fill in the group)

If you don't have a ritual for moving into a new home or office . . .

Moving is one of life's passages, not unlike reaching adolescence or getting married. A new environment offers a context for possibilities that can renew, refresh, and remodel your life. Ceremonies surrounding rites of passage serve to highlight and sanctify change. A ceremony significantly deepens the connection to each event.

This year I attended my son's inauguration into medical school. What a wonderful experience Wayne State University provides its students by distinguishing this lifetime commitment to healing with a convocation ceremony.

The only cure for not having a ritual is to create one. Ask family members to write a poem or message and share them together. Have a festive picnic, even if it needs to be held inside. Join together and take a ceremonial walk around the property's perimeter or have each member of a family place a flower in a vase on a window's ledge. Simply stop and take time to honor the transition between the past and the possibilities for the future.

31

MODERN LIFE

Like soothing an itch, we scratch away at the surface of discontentment without obliterating it. Pervasive modern-day ills lie not so much in what we have not but in what we feel not. The cause for our dissatisfaction has been expressed in the infamous Unabomber's written plea. He attributes the social and psychological problems of modern society to the fact that society requires people to live under conditions radically different from those under which the human race evolved. On some level this grievance seems on the mark.

What is the root of such feelings? Why does our life seem to be out of sync with our needs? Since we are the creators of our life, why don't we honor our intrinsic needs?

A field of science called *evolutionary psychology* has some answers. In what's called the *mismatch theory* our present environment is contrasted with the one in which we were designed to function. Life today is not in accord with our adaptive genetic traits. We were not designed to live removed from social interaction, filling our time with attention to artificially created items. Sitting in front of a computer, in a factory bolting together some widget, or performing a service to paper and numbers, sealed in a high-rise office, was not in the cards in our original design. We were not meant to sit stationary all day, to use our eyes only for close-range purposes, or to be separated from fresh air and sunlight.

Human beings are part of a system of life that depends on every facet to thrive. If we look deeply within, we know we are best off when at one with our surroundings.

Consider how dramatically we are influenced by our environment. Like the tale of the goldfish that grows as big as the body of water, we expand to the limit of our spaces, physically and emotionally. Raise children with love, and they shall be loving. Provide a space to experiment and pursue interests, and we will become satisfied, scintillating people. It is the exception rather than the rule to be able to circumvent the influence exerted on us from our surroundings.

Feng shui professionals in the pyramid school must make a pledge, much like the Hippocratic oath of physicians. In it we are told to empty ourselves so we can receive information unimpeded by self. Experience the space around you with an unfiltered mind. Only when we are empty can we be filled.

The cures for our individual lives can be retrieved from a knowledge of how to integrate our lives with our surroundings. Only when we focus on modifying our environment to support the best for our lives will some distressing areas of our lives fall away gently, naturally, and irrevocably, like fall leaves on their pilgrimage toward extinction.

Afterword

Ah, the whim of chance.

The heavy exacting combination of matter that we are is as capricious as a role of dice. Along the path to existence, the slightest variation would have hatched us in another form. One altered speck of chromosome, one fleeting break of DNA would deliver an entirely different configuration to life. Even our galaxy, seen as fiercely immutable, is as fragile as an orchid's bloom carved in ice flying past the sun.

How then can we not be humbled when contemplating what must be in order to thrive? Know fortune has tipped its hand in configuring the world as it is today. What separates us from oblivion is merely a few shifts in structure. We are what is around us and were almost not.

Appreciate the miracle of now, but love it lightly.

Bibliography

Alexander, Christopher, et al. *A Pattern Language: Towns, Buildings, Construction*. Oxford: Oxford University Press, 1977.

Becker, R. O., and Gary Selden. *The Body Electric*. New York: William Morrow, 1985.

Blake, Peter. *No Place like Utopia*. New York: Alfred A. Knopf, 1993.

Craze, Richard. *Feng Shui for Beginners*. London: Hodder & Stoughton, 1995.

Dagens, Bruno. *Mayamata: An Indian Treatise on Housing, Architecture and Iconography*. New Delhi, India: Sitaram Bhartia Institute of Scientific Research, 1985.

Das, Potluru Krishna. *The Secrets of Vastu*. Sikh Village, Secunderabad: Udayalakshmi Publications, 1989.

Eitel, Ernest J. *Feng Shui: The Science of Sacred Landscape in Old China*. Tucson, Arizona: Synergetic Press, 1984.

Fairchild, Dennis. *Healing Homes*. Birmingham, Michigan: Wavefield Books, 1996.

Gallagher, Winifred. *The Power of Place*. New York: Simon and Schuster, 1993.

Govert, John Dennis. *Feng Shui: Art and Harmony of Place*. Phoenix, Arizona: Daikakuji Publications, 1993.

Groves, Derham. *Feng Shui and Western Building Ceremonies*. Singapore: Graham Brash, 1991.

Hall, Edward T. *The Hidden Dimension*. New York: Anchor Books, Doubleday, 1966.

Hall, Edward T. *The Silent Language*. New York: Doubleday, 1973.

Hiss, Tony. *The Experience of Place*. New York: Alfred A. Knopf, 1990.

Jacobs, Jane. *Cities and the Wealth of Nations*. New York: Vintage Books, Random House, Inc., 1985.

Kaplan, Stephen & Rachel. *Cognition and Environment*. Ann Arbor, Michigan: Ulrich's Bookstore, 1983.

Lam, William. *Perception and Light as Formgivers to Architecture*. New York: McGraw-Hill, 1977.

Lawlor, Robert. *Sacred Geometry*. New York: Crossroad Publishing Company, 1982.

MacKaye, Benton. *The New Exploration: A Philosophy of Regional Planning*. Champaign, Illinois: University of Illinois Press, 1962.

Marfori, Mark D. *Feng Shui: Discover Money, Health and Love*. Santa Monica, California: Dragon Publishing, 1993.

O'Brien, Joanne. *The Elements of Feng Shui*. Great Britain: Element Books Ltd., 1991.

Rossbach, Sarah. *Feng Shui: The Chinese Art of Placement*. New York: E. P. Dutton, 1983.

Rossbach, Sarah. *Interior Design with Feng Shui*. New York: E. P. Dutton, 1987.

Rybczynski, Witold. *The Most Beautiful House in the World*. New York: Penguin Group, 1990.

Sennet, Richard. *The Conscience of the Eye*. New York: W. W. Norton Co., 1990.

Spear, William. *Feng Shui Made Easy*. New York: HarperCollins Publications, 1995.

Swan, James. *Bound to the Earth*. New York: Avon, 1994.

Thompson, Angel. *Feng Shui, The Art of Attraction*. New York: St. Martins Press, 1996.

Walters, Derek. *Feng Shui*. New York: Simon and Schuster, 1988.

Waters, Derek. *The Feng Shui Handbook: A Practical Guide to Chinese Geomancy and Environmental Harmony*. London: The Aquarian Press, 1991.

Wydra, Nancilee. *Feng Shui, Designing Your Happiness, A Contemporary Look at Feng Shui*. Torrance, California: Heian International, 1995.

Index

Note: Italicized entries indicate illustrations.